Jesus on Trial

Jesus on Trial

by
John MacArthur, Jr.

MOODY PRESS
CHICAGO

All Scripture quotations, unless noted otherwise, are from the *New Scofield Reference Bible*, King James Version. Copyright © 1967 by Oxford University Press, Inc. Reprinted by permission.

Library of Congress Cataloging in Publication Data

MacArthur, John, 1939-
    Jesus on trial.

    (John MacArthur Bible studies)
    1. Bible. N.T. Matthew XXVI, 31-75—Criticism, interpretation, etc. 2. Jesus Christ—Passion.
I. Title. II. Series: MacArthur, John, 1939-
Bible studies.
BS2575.2.M245 1988   232.9'62   87-31525
ISBN 0-8024-5355-4

1 2 3 4 5 6 7 Printing/LC/Year 93 92 91 90 89 88

Printed in the United States of America

Contents

These Bible studies are taken from messages delivered by Pastor-Teacher John MacArthur, Jr., at Grace Community Church in Panorama City, California. The recorded messages themselves may be purchased as a series or individually. Please request the current price list by writing to:

WORD OF GRACE COMMUNICATIONS
P.O. Box 4000
Panorama City, CA 91412

Or call the following toll-free number:
1-800-55-GRACE

1
Restoring Deserting Disciples

Outline

Introduction
A. The Significance of the Lesson on Weakness
   1. Predicting the desertion of the disciples
   2. Preserving the majesty of Christ
B. The Setting of the Lesson on Weakness
   1. Imparting the legacy
   2. Departing from the upper room

Lesson
 I. A Contrast Between Knowledge and Ignorance
   A. The Ignorance of the Disciples
   B. The Knowledge of Christ
      1. The panoramic view of Christ
      2. The prophetic plan of God
         a) The context of Zechariah 13:7
         b) The interpretation of Zechariah 13:7
            (1) Identifying the shepherd
            (2) Identifying the sheep
 II. A Contrast Between Courage and Cowardice
   A. The Cowardice of the Disciples
   B. The Courage of Christ
III. A Contrast Between Power and Weakness
   A. Jesus' Power over Death
      1. Christ's commitment to God's power
      2. The disciples' distrust of God's power
   B. Jesus' Promise Regarding His Death

Introduction

A. The Significance of the Lesson on Weakness

As much as we like to think of ourselves as strong Christians, we are in fact weak. We like to believe we could never be caught in a situation where we would deny the Lord or His Word. But the truth is that there are times when we deny Him. There are times when we desert Christ to avoid embarrassment or shame. And so it was with Jesus' disciples.

1. Predicting the desertion of the disciples

The lesson Christ teaches the disciples in Matthew 26:31-35 is beneficial for us as well. Jesus predicted that the disciples would desert Him—and it came to pass exactly as He said. That profound and unforgettable lesson changed the course of their lives. Of all that Jesus could have taught the disciples, He chose to reveal their weakness through predicting their future desertion. Matthew, under the direction of the Holy Spirit, placed that prediction in the midst of his treatment of Christ's preparation for the cross. To carry the gospel to the world, the disciples had to be strong. But the first step to acquiring strength was admitting weakness. A lesson on weakness was vital for the disciples.

The disciples affirmed their commitment to Christ on the basis of their own strength. They believed their love for Christ, spiritual strength, and ability to control Satan was greater than it actually was. They were leaning on their own understanding (cf. Prov. 3:5). When Christ was taken captive in the garden, the moment came for them to take a stand for Christ. Matthew said, "Then all the disciples forsook him, and fled" (Matt. 26:56). The promise Peter and the rest of the disciples make in verse 35 is empty because it is based on human strength. Jesus had to teach the disciples a lesson about the inadequacy of their own strength in the midst of spiritual warfare.

2. Preserving the majesty of Christ

Matthew was not focusing primarily on the disciples, although they were the surface issue. His primary objective was to preserve the majesty of Jesus Christ. How could Christ retain dignity, respect, and glory amid the desertion and defection of His followers? What kind of leader is He whose troops desert Him during the heat of battle? Lesser men than the disciples have been in more severe circumstances yet stood their ground. Did Christ choose the wrong men? Such accusations potentially demean and weaken Christ's regal splendor. But Matthew, under the inspiration of the Holy Spirit, exalts Christ by contrasting Him to the defecting disciples. The majestic character of Jesus Christ is presented as clearly in this passage as in any other in the New Testament.

B. The Setting of the Lesson on Weakness

The time in Matthew 26:31 is hours before the crucifixion. Christ was approaching the conclusion of His earthly life and the climax of redemptive history. Only four chapters in all four gospels are devoted to the first thirty years of Christ's life, yet thirteen are devoted to the last day of His life. In preparation for the cross, Christ closed the Old Covenant with His final Passover, instituting the New Covenant of His body and His blood, which was represented by the bread and cup of the Lord's Supper.

9

1. Imparting the legacy

   Matthew 26:30 says, "When they had sung an hymn,
   they went out into the Mount of Olives." During the
   Passover meal, Jesus and His disciples consumed four
   cups of wine. After the main meal—consisting of the
   Passover lamb, bitter herbs and sauce, and unleavened
   bread—they drank the third cup and sang the latter por-
   tion of the Hallel (Psalm 115-18). Then they drank the
   last cup and sang the final song—Psalm 136, the Great
   Hallel. Every verse in Psalm 136 ends with the phrase
   "for his mercy endureth forever."

   Matthew left something out of his narrative. Before they
   sing the last hymn, Jesus teaches His disciples the things
   recorded in John 14-16 and prays the prayer recorded in
   John 17. In the three chapters of teaching, Jesus promises to pass on His legacy to the disciples—His gifts of
   peace, joy, contentment, comfort, the Holy Spirit, the
   Word of God, and hope for the future. He spoke of the
   persecution to come but promised ultimate deliverance.
   Then Jesus prayed to the Father for the unity of all His
   disciples, including those who would come to believe in
   Him in the days ahead. We know those things happened before they left the upper room because John 18:1
   says, "When Jesus had spoken these words, he went
   forth with his disciples."

2. Departing from the upper room

   When Jesus and the disciples left the upper room it was
   nearly midnight. As they went out into the street, they
   saw the city alive with activity, as if it were midday. It
   was the time of the Passover—the feast of unleavened
   bread. Some people were eating their Passover meal,
   such as the Galileans and the Pharisees. Some were still
   preparing to eat it the next day, such as the Judeans and
   the Sadducees. The Temple gates were opened at midnight for the festival, and many people were surging toward it. Visitors to Jerusalem were everywhere, negoti-
   ating for a place to hold their Passover. Many people
   were carrying the animals they would sacrifice the next
   day.

It was through such activity that Jesus and the disciples passed. Once they were out of the city, they went down the eastern slope of the Temple mount and crossed the Kidron brook, running full with water from the winter rains and with the blood of thousands of animals slain in the Temple. The blood flowed out the back of the Temple, down the slope, and into the brook. After crossing the brook they ascended the Mount of Olives to their familiar resting place—the Garden of Gethsemane (Gethsemane probably meant "olive press"). People didn't own gardens in the city—there was no room. But they could maintain gardens on the slopes of the hills around the city.

There were only eleven disciples with Jesus; the Lord had dismissed Judas several hours before. As Jesus and the disciples ascended the Mount of Olives, they needed to stop and rest. While they rested, Jesus confronted the disciples about their weaknesses.

Jesus' teaching prior to this time had basically been positive—they received nothing but promises in John 13-16. But now it was time for a warning. They needed to learn that strength is born out of a recognition of weakness, not a recognition of strength. Jesus intended to eliminate illusions. As He taught that lesson we see a marvelous contrast between Christ and His defecting disciples.

Lesson

I. A CONTRAST BETWEEN KNOWLEDGE AND IGNORANCE

A. The Ignorance of the Disciples

The disciples were woefully ignorant. Peter said, "Though all men shall be offended because of thee, yet will I never be offended" (Matt. 26:33). In only a few hours they all defected, including Peter. In verse 35 Peter says, "Though I should die with thee, yet will I not deny thee." The rest of the verse says that all the disciples affirmed the same thing. They were all ignorant of their own weaknesses and the strength of Satan. They were ignorant of the power of the test they would face in a few hours. They were ignorant of many things, to say nothing of their ignorance of the Old Testament, including the prophecy of Zechariah 13:7 referred to by Christ in verse 31: "I will smite the shepherd, and the sheep of the flock shall be scattered abroad."

B. The Knowledge of Christ

In contrast to the ignorance of the disciples is the knowledge of Jesus Christ. Beginning in verse 31 Jesus teaches the disciples a lesson about the stupidity of self-sufficiency. He said, "All ye shall be offended because of me this night; for it is written, I will smite the shepherd, and the sheep of the flock shall be scattered abroad. But after I am raised up again, I will go before you into Galilee" (vv. 31-32). Then in verse 34 Jesus says to Peter, "Verily I say unto thee that this night, before the cock crows, thou shalt deny me thrice." Jesus knew the disciples would forsake Him that night. Nevertheless, He knew He would be raised from the dead and would meet them again in Galilee.

1. The panoramic view of Christ

Jesus could see what Judas was doing at that exact moment. He could see the Jewish rulers planning their strategy. He could see Peter's denial and the disciples fleeing from His presence. He could see the Roman soldiers and Jewish leaders coming with clubs, swords, and torches into the garden to take Him captive. He could see the kiss of Judas Iscariot on His cheek. With the eyes of His supernatural knowledge He saw the prophecies of the Old Testament vividly coming to pass. He could see the plan of God unfolding. Jesus didn't strain to acquire such knowledge; it was easily within His grasp.

Nothing was lost of Jesus' regal majesty. It remained clear because His knowledge of those events was clear. He knew what would happen that very night. He knew the past—for it was written in the plan of God. And He knew the future—that the disciples would forsake Him.

2. The prophetic plan of God

One of the reasons Jesus knew what was going to happen was that He knew Scripture. In Matthew 26:31 Jesus says, "All ye shall be offended because of me this night; for it is written." What was about to take place was in the plan of God. It was not some event initiated by the whim and will of Judas, the religious leaders, or anyone else on earth. It was God's divine plan. Jesus quotes Zechariah 13:7 in Matthew 26:31: "I will smite the shepherd, and the sheep of the flock shall be scattered abroad." Jesus knew not only what Judas and the religious leaders were doing but also what Satan was planning. Jesus knew how all the events of that night and next morning would turn out because of His knowledge of the past, present, and future.

a) The context of Zechariah 13:7

Zechariah 13:7 is not an easy passage to interpret. If it had been simple, the disciples might have understood it. The context speaks of false prophets, whom God will judge according to their false prophecies. Then verse 7 says, "Smite the shepherd, and the sheep shall be scattered."

b) The interpretation of Zechariah 13:7

At first it might seem that the Lord is referring to smiting a false shepherd and scattering his followers. But we have the clear interpretation of Christ, who says that the smitten shepherd is the Messiah and the scattered flock His people.

(1) Identifying the shepherd

In Zechariah 13:7 God says, "Awake, O sword, against my shepherd." That statement indicates that God is not referring to a false prophet. God wouldn't refer to a false prophet as His shepherd or personal representative. God said He would bring His sword "against the man." Here Zechariah uses a Hebrew word that is not the generic

13

word for man but one that means "mighty man" or "man of great strength." The shepherd God would slay is the mighty shepherd of God. Verse 7 says, "The man who is my fellow." That literally means "the mighty man of My union" or "the mighty man equal to Me." Who is equal to God? Who was God's Shepherd? Who is the mighty Shepherd? Christ. Clearly Zechariah has turned from a discussion of false shepherds. Although it was true that God would wound the false shepherd in the house of his idol (v. 6), God would also wound the true Shepherd and scatter His sheep. The end of verse 7 says, "I will turn mine hand upon the little ones." That means God will preserve a remnant.

(2) Identifying the sheep

Zechariah was saying that the day was coming when God was going to smite His own Shepherd, the Lord Jesus Christ, and scatter the sheep. I believe Zechariah was referring to the nation Israel. Israel was characterized by chaos after the death of their Messiah. In A.D. 70 the city of Jerusalem was destroyed along with the Temple. Today the Jewish people are experiencing that same chaos as a result of rejecting their Messiah. The scattering of the disciples was the first phase of that chaos. But Zechariah 13:7 also says, "I will turn mine hand upon the little ones." When the nation of Israel went into chaos, God gathered the scattered disciples. (Many Christians were preserved from the destruction of Jerusalem in A.D. 70 because they fled [cf. Luke 19:20-22].) Similarly, God will preserve a future remnant of those who love Christ.

The prophecy of Zechariah is critical to our understanding of Christ's supernatural knowledge. He knew the meaning of the plan of God. He knew how to interpret a difficult passage in Zechariah perfectly and clearly. He understood the disciples— He knew what they were going to do. He knew what Satan was going to bring to bear on them, and He knew they wouldn't handle it. He knew what Peter would do, even though he said he wouldn't do it. He knew every detail of what was going to happen and when. Jesus didn't lose, but the disciples did. They were not heroes—they abandoned Christ. They revealed themselves to be ignorant, unable to understand the plan of God, the prophetic word, or the signs of the times. Christ shines by comparison.

II. A CONTRAST BETWEEN COURAGE AND COWARDICE

A. The Cowardice of the Disciples

Matthew 26:31 says, "All ye shall be offended." The Greek word translated "offended" means "trapped." The disciples were going to be caught in a trap—one they couldn't escape.

What was the trap? Proverbs 29:25 says, "The fear of man bringeth a snare." The disciples were afraid of what the Romans or Jewish leaders would do to them. When they saw the soldiers and leaders come with clubs, staves, and swords to seize Christ, they fled. They defected in the heat of battle. It happened exactly as Christ said. When the pressure mounted, they fled. They were ashamed to be identified with Christ and bear His reproach. They loved Him and desired to be faithful, but they were afraid.

The disciples didn't have faith to believe the Lord could deliver them from their trial. They saw Christ as a victim. But if Christ were a victim, what were they going to be? If He couldn't escape from the soldiers, how would they escape? Admittedly, identifying one's self with Jesus Christ can bring reproach. Hebrews 11:26 says Moses esteemed "the reproach of Christ greater riches than the treasures in Egypt." But everyone doesn't make that choice. There are some who flee when the pressure is on, running for safety because they're afraid.

B. The Courage of Christ

In contrast to the cowardice of the disciples is the perfect courage of Christ. He steadfastly moved toward the cross, committing Himself to the Father's will. Christ trusted the Father and put His life in His hands. The disciples couldn't do that. They were cowards. Christ's valor is remarkable.

15

He was going to the cross to bear the sins of the world, even though He'd never been touched by sin. He would be abused, mocked, and spat on, yet He moved toward His fate with distinctly divine valor. His courage was predicated on an absolute trust in the Father, who commissioned Him for such a purpose.

Even defecting disciples couldn't diminish the majesty of the Lord. They fled out of fear, but He stood true to His task with great courage, facing death, sin, and Satan for their sake.

III. A CONTRAST BETWEEN POWER AND WEAKNESS

A. Jesus' Power over Death

The disciples were afraid to face the moment of their trial because they were weak and couldn't handle death. In Matthew 26:32 the Lord says, "After I am raised up again, I will go before you into Galilee." The Lord faced death with great courage because He knew He had power over death. The disciples knew they didn't, but they wouldn't commit themselves to the One who did. They lacked faith.

1. Christ's commitment to God's power

Romans 6:4 says that Christ "was raised up from the dead by the glory of the Father." Before Jesus went to the grave, He repeatedly said He would be raised from the dead (Matt. 16:21; 17:9; 20:19). He committed Himself to God's divine power over death. Hebrews 2:14-15 says "that through death he might destroy him that had the power of death, that is, the devil, and deliver them who, through fear of death, were all their lifetime subject to bondage." Christ was able to face the cross because He knew He had the power to conquer death. He took on death as an enemy to be defeated. The disciples paled in comparison.

Christ believed what Abraham believed when he offered up Isaac. Hebrews 11:19 says that Abraham knew "God was able to raise him [Isaac] up." Abraham believed that if God wanted to take Isaac's life, He would have to raise him from the dead to fulfill His promise. That's why he was willing to offer up his son. And

16

that's why Christ was willing to go to the grave: He knew God fulfilled His promises. In Christ's case, God promised to raise Him from the dead to make Him King of kings.

2. The disciples' distrust of God's power

The disciples should have known that God would raise up Christ. After all, only a few days prior they saw Jesus raise Lazarus from the dead (John 11:44). Even the rulers knew He raised Lazarus. The disciples should have remembered that Jesus said, "I am the resurrection, and the life; he that believeth in me, though he were dead, yet shall he live. And whosoever liveth and believeth in me shall never die. Believest thou this?" (John 11:25-26). But in the weakness of their faith, they remained cowards. In the strength of His commitment to God, Jesus moved toward the cross with power.

The majesty of Christ shines in comparison to the weakness of the disciples. He believed in the power of God over death; they did not.

B. Jesus' Promise Regarding His Death

Jesus told the disciples He would go before them into Galilee (Matt. 26:32). He would return to be their Shepherd and lead them once again. And He did just that. After being raised from the dead, He told Mary Magdalene and the other Mary, "Go tell my brethren that they go into Galilee, and there shall they see me" (Matt. 28:10). He came out of the grave and kept His appointment with the disciples. He knew He had the power not only to conquer death but also to abolish death. But the disciples had weak faith, love, and gratitude.

This lesson is important for us to learn. We parade our ignorance when we boast about our courage, for when the chips are down we may turn out to be cowards. We can claim to have strength to face any test, but when the test arrives we so often find ourselves to be weak. Yet that's not all bad. Until you learn you are weak, you can't know where true strength lies. In 2 Corinthians 12:9 Paul quotes the Lord's instruction to

17

him: "My strength is made perfect in weakness." We must all learn to stop trusting in ourselves.

IV. A CONTRAST BETWEEN PRIDE AND HUMILITY

Matthew 26:33 says, "Peter answered and said unto him, Though all men shall be offended because of thee, yet will I never be offended." Peter was claiming to be the most trustworthy disciple of all. He was proud and self-confident but also weak and ignorant.

A. Predictions of Peter's Denials

1. John 13:38

Peter didn't learn his lessons well. It was only a few hours before that the Lord confronted his boasting. While they were in the upper room, the Lord and Peter entered into this dialogue: "Simon Peter said unto him, Lord, where goest thou? Jesus answered him, Where I go, thou canst not follow me now; but thou shalt follow me afterwards. Peter said unto him, Lord, why cannot I follow thee now? I will lay down my life for thy sake. Jesus answered him, Wilt thou lay down thy life for my sake? Verily, verily, I say unto thee, The cock shall not crow, till thou hast denied me thrice" (John 13:36-38).

2. Matthew 26:34

Later that night, after Jesus and the disciples left the upper room and were resting on a slope of the Mount of Olives, Peter claimed, "Though all men shall be offended because of thee, yet will I never be offended" (Matt. 26:33). In verse 34 Jesus gives Peter the same answer He did in John 13:38: "Verily I say unto thee that this night, before the cock crows, thou shalt deny me thrice." Twice in one night Peter was told of his coming denials, yet he remained prideful and self-confident.

3. Luke 22:34

Luke's gospel records the first occurrence of Jesus' prediction, and Luke provides greater detail than John. Jesus said, "Simon, Simon, behold, Satan hath desired to have you, that he may sift you as wheat" (Luke 22:31). Sifting is the process of separating the wheat from the chaff by violent shaking. In the phrase "Satan wants to have *you*," Luke used the Greek word *humas*. It is plural; Satan wanted to shake all the disciples as they had never been shaken before.

Peter had a previous encounter with Satan. In Matthew 16:22 Peter rebukes Christ for predicting His coming death. Jesus then said to Peter, "Get thee behind me, Satan" (v. 23). This present circumstance was not a new one for Peter.

Jesus did not leave His prediction without encouragement. In Luke 22:32 He says, "I have prayed for thee, that thy faith fail not. And when thou art converted, strengthen thy brethren." Jesus prayed that Peter and the other disciples would not experience a total collapse. They would be restored and would then be able to strengthen others because they would have learned the lesson of not trusting in themselves.

In spite of that encouragement, Peter remained resolute in his obstinacy: "Lord, I am ready to go with thee, both into prison, and to death" (v. 33). Then the Lord said, "Peter, the cock shall not crow this day, before that thou shalt thrice deny that thou knowest me" (v. 34).

Manifestations of Peter's Pride

Peter and the rest of the disciples stood on treacherous ground. Frankly, Peter was acting like a fool. His foolish pride was manifest in three ways.

1. He contradicted the Lord

Contradicting a superior is a serious matter. Peter was actually saying that the Lord of the universe was wrong when he insisted that he wouldn't deny Him.

2. He claimed superiority over the other disciples

In Matthew 26:33 Peter says, "Though all men shall be offended because of thee, yet will I never be offended."

3. He trusted in his own strength

In verse 35 he says, "Though I should die with thee, yet will I not deny thee. Likewise also said all the disciples."

B. Pain over Peter's Denials

1. Experienced by Christ

The humility of Jesus is revealed beautifully in verse 34: "This night, before the cock crows, thou shalt deny me thrice." At that point Jesus would be alone—forsaken and deserted. The majestic, humble Christ resolutely and willingly went to the cross to die and shed His blood for weak and proud disciples, who deserted Him at a time He needed them most. What amazing condescension and humility! How dare they be ashamed of the living God, who is not ashamed of them! It is understandable for God to be ashamed to associate with sinners but inexcusable for sinners to be ashamed to associate with God.

The Time of the Denials

In Matthew 26:34 the Lord pinpointed the time of Peter's denials: "This night, before the cock crows." The Jews divided the night into four parts: evening (6:00 P.M. to 9:00 P.M.), midnight (9:00 P.M. to midnight), cock crow (midnight to 3:00 A.M.), and morning (3:00 A.M. to 6:00 A.M.). The period from midnight to 3:00 A.M. was called cockcrow because that's the approximate time roosters crowed. It was nearly midnight when, for the second time, the Lord predicted Peter's denials. In a few hours, before three in the morning, Peter would deny the Lord three times.

2. Experienced by Peter

> Christ knew every detail of what would happen, not only regarding His own life but Peter's as well. He knew where Peter would be, whom he would meet, and how he would deny Him.
>
> The setting of Peter's denials took place in the courtyard of the high priest's residence. While Peter waited to see what would happen to Jesus, he was confronted by people about his association with Christ. According to Matthew 26:74 Peter begins "to curse and to swear." Peter not only denied Christ; he was profane in his denial. Then he said, "I know not the man. And immediately the cock crowed. And Peter remembered the word of Jesus" (vv. 74-75). What a painful remembrance! Verse 75 concludes, "He went out, and wept bitterly." Peter remembered having said, "Though I should die with thee, yet will I not deny thee" (v. 35). It was a nice sentiment, but Peter didn't have the strength to pull it off.
>
> Luke adds a poignant detail to this narrative: "Peter said, Man, I know not what thou sayest. And immediately, while he yet spoke, the cock crowed. And the Lord turned, and looked on Peter" (22:60-61). Can you imagine how Peter must have felt?

We see the pride of the disciples in sharp contrast to the humility of Christ, who was to sacrifice Himself for those who wouldn't name His name under pressure.

V. A CONTRAST BETWEEN DESERTION AND RESTORATION

A. The Promise of Restoration

> Matthew 26:32 leads us to the positive conclusion of the matter. Jesus said, "After I am raised up again, I will go before you into Galilee." The idea is that He would lead them into Galilee. In spite of the disciples' deserting the Lord, He was loving and merciful. He restored them. He lived out the repeated phrase "his mercy endureth forever" in Psalm 136. The disciples were worthy of nothing, yet in spite of what they did He gathered them together and led them into Galilee. John 21:15-17 records His specific resto-

ration of Peter. Christ asked Peter to feed His sheep. Three times He asked him if he loved Him, as if to make up for the three times Peter denied Him. Once He restored all the disciples to the task of the ministry, He ascended into heaven, gave them the Holy Spirit, and sent them out to change the world.

B. The Proof of Restoration

Christ's restoration of the disciples proves to me that God is in the business of restoring those who have deserted Him. That's comforting to know. We as believers may forsake Him at some point in our lives, but under no condition will He ever forsake us.

Jesus said, "Without me ye can do nothing" (John 15:5). You must learn that your resources are in the Lord, not in your own strength. The disciples learned that lesson. Acts 5:41-42 proves it. A council of Jewish leaders in Jerusalem called in the apostles for questioning regarding their activities. They beat the apostles and "commanded that they should not speak in the name of Jesus, and let them go" (v. 40). Those apostles, with the exception of one, were the same men who deserted our Lord in Matthew 26:56. You might expect them to run again. But Acts 5:41-42 says, "They departed from the presence of the council, rejoicing that they were counted worthy to suffer shame for his [Jesus'] name. And daily in the temple, and in every house, they ceased not to teach and preach Jesus Christ."

Conclusion

The disciples learned a powerful lesson about their weakness. Jesus returned from the grave and put His loving arms around them, restoring them. He then recommissioned them and sent them out. After seeing His mercy and power in His resurrection, they were no longer afraid of death. They knew they also would rise from the dead. The grace of Christ left them to go out with a new approach. The same thing must be true in our lives. Not until we realize how the sweet and tender grace of the Lord has restored us will we go out and conquer the difficulties we will surely face. I thank God for the times I failed and the Lord taught me the frailty of my own strength. But I can rest with the knowledge that my strength is only in His power.

Focusing on the Facts

1. Why did Jesus need to teach the disciples a lesson on weakness (see p. 8)?
2. What is Matthew's focus in Matthew 26:31-35? What accusation was he attempting to defuse (see p. 9)?
3. What event did Matthew leave out of his narrative that John included (see p. 10)?
4. In what ways were the disciples ignorant (see pp. 11-12)?
5. What were some of the events that Christ saw before they took place (see p. 12)?
6. How did Christ know what was going to happen (Matt. 26:31; see p. 13)?
7. What is the context of Zechariah 13:7? How did Christ interpret that verse (see p. 13)?
8. Who is the shepherd referred to in Zechariah 13:7? Explain. Who are the sheep? Explain (see pp. 13-14).
9. What trap did the disciples fall into (Prov. 29:25; see p. 15)?
10. How was Christ's courage manifested (see pp. 15-16)?
11. Why was Christ able to face the cross with courage (see p. 16)?
12. The disciples could have faced death with courage if they had remembered what event (see pp. 16-17)?
13. On how many occasions did Christ predict Peter's denials (see p. 18)?
14. In what way did Christ encourage the disciples in the midst of predicting their coming denial (see p. 19)?
15. In what three ways did Peter manifest his pride (see pp. 19-20)?
16. How is the humility of Christ revealed in His prediction of Peter's denials (see p. 20)?
17. When did the Lord predict that Peter would deny Him (see p. 20)?
18. How did Christ restore the disciples (see pp. 21-22)?
19. What does Christ's restoration of the disciples prove about God (see p. 22)?

Pondering the Principles

1. The disciples deserted Christ because they were afraid of what the Roman and Jewish leaders would do to them. And that fear translates as being ashamed of Christ. Does your behavior betray your shame of being identified with Christ? When you are in a situation that calls for you to identify with Christ, do you keep quiet—or even deny Him? If you have been guilty of being ashamed of Christ, confess that now. As an act of repentance, you can turn your fear of people into courage. Look at how Christ faced the cross. He put His complete trust in God. You need to do the same. That means you have to risk being vulnerable to abuse and suffering, but that is God's will for your life (1 Pet. 3:17). To help in times of suffering, memorize 2 Timothy 3:12: "All who desire to live godly in Christ Jesus will be persecuted" (NASB*).

2. Peter manifested his pride in three ways: he contradicted the Lord, claimed superiority over the other disciples, and trusted in his own strength. Have you been guilty of that kind of pride? Look up the following verses: Romans 12:3; 1 Corinthians 10:12; Philippians 2:3, 9-11. How do each of those passages apply to the three manifestations of pride? Based on those verses, what should your attitude be towards the Lord, other believers, and yourself? Commit yourself to a daily pursuit of those attitudes.

New American Standard Bible.

2

The Son in Sorrow—Part 1

Outline

Introduction

Lesson
I. Setting the Scene (vv. 36-37*a*)
   A. The Time
      1. Reviewing Christ's prediction
      2. Reviewing Passover week
   B. The Place
   C. The People
      1. Establishing the guard
         a) An important opportunity
         b) An intense objective
      2. Instructing the leaders
         a) Christ's reason for choosing the three
            (1) Companionship
            (2) Observation
            (3) Instruction
         b) Christ's skill in conveying a lesson
         c) Christ's remedy for facing a temptation
            (1) What sinless humanity acknowledges
            (2) What sinless humanity feels
II. Unfolding the Text (vv. 37*b*-46)
   A. Sorrow (vv. 37*b*-38)
      1. The essence of Christ's sorrow (v. 37*b*)
         a) The anticipation of the cross
         b) The agony of depression
         c) The attack of Satan
            (1) His method
            (2) His motive
      2. The extent of Christ's sorrow (v. 38)

B. Supplication (vv. 39, 42, 44)
 1. The first supplication (v. 39)
  a) The elements of Christ's prayer
   (1) His comfort in God's love
   (2) His conflict over God's plan
   (3) His consumption of God's wrath
   (4) His commitment to God's will

Introduction

The hymn "Hallelujah, What a Savior!" written by Phillip Bliss begins,

> "Man of sorrows!" what a name
> For the Son of God, who came
> Ruined sinners to reclaim!
> Hallelujah, what a Savior!

The phrase "man of sorrows" is taken from Isaiah 53:3, which says the Messiah would be "a man of sorrows, and acquainted with grief." The Lord was a man of sorrows. There is no record in Scripture of Jesus ever laughing, but there are many statements about His grief. In John 11:35 He weeps over the grave of Lazarus. Prior to that He groaned deep within Himself when He saw the impact of sin and death (v. 33). And as Jesus looked over the city of Jerusalem, He wept over its evil and unbelieving population (Luke 19:41).

Yet none of Christ's sorrow over disease, unbelief, disobedience, ignorance, or rejection can compare to what He experiences in Matthew 26:36-46. The sorrow He experienced in the Garden of Gethsemane was an accumulation and intensification of all the sorrow He had ever known in His life. To study the suffering of Jesus in this text is like treading on holy ground. We will attempt to explain something that is inexplicable. It is mystery too profound for mortal man and perhaps even the holy angels. We stand in awe of the God-man—fully aware of His deity—yet see Him suffer pain, as if He were not God. It is too much for us to understand.

Matthew 26:36-46 is powerful. The Lord was in the Garden of Gethsemane, prior to His capture, mock trial, and execution. This passage details one aspect of His preparation for the cross. But it also prepares the disciples. Although Christ had to endure His struggle in the garden to fulfill God's plan to defeat the devil, it also is an important element in the disciples' preparation. Out of that experience they would learn the profound lesson of verse 41, where our Lord says, "Watch and pray, that ye enter not into temptation; the spirit indeed is willing, but the flesh is weak." Ever and always the teacher, even in the midst of an unbelievable and inexplicable struggle with the enemy, the Lord saw beyond His own experience to teach His own. In His struggle He saw a great lesson—one that teaches us how we should face temptation and severe trials.

To see our way through this narrative and to draw a poignant conclusion, I want to give you five key words: sorrow, supplication, sleep, strength, and sequence. But before we look at them, we need to establish the context of this passage.

Lesson

I. SETTING THE SCENE (vv. 36-37a)

"Then cometh Jesus with them unto a place called Gethsemane, and saith unto the disciples, Sit here, while I go and pray yonder. And he took with him Peter and the two sons of Zebedee."

A. The Time

1. Reviewing Christ's prediction

"Then" sets up a chronological flow. It places us just after the Lord predicted the disciples' denial and desertion. They denied they would ever do such a thing, but they did, just as Christ said.

2. Reviewing Passover week

The setting is midnight on Thursday of the last week of our Lord's life. His few years of ministry are complete. The Galilean, Judean, and Perean ministries, along with miracles and healings, have ended. It is now the Passover in Jerusalem in the year A.D. 33 or A.D. 30 (depending on which date is used for Christ's birth). He came not only to attend the Passover but also to be the Passover. On Saturday He arrived in Bethany to stay with His friends Mary, Martha, and Lazarus. On Sunday crowds came to Bethany to hear Him teach. On Monday He rode into the city of Jerusalem to the hosannas and praises of the people, who proclaimed Him as their Messiah. On Tuesday He cleansed the Temple. On Wednesday He entered the Temple and both taught the people and rebuked the religious leaders. On Wednesday evening He ascended the Mount of Olives and taught the disciples about His second coming. On Thursday Peter and John made preparations for the Passover, and that evening Christ and His disciples ate the Passover meal.

The time was now near midnight. Christ and the disciples finished the meal, sang the final hymn, and left the upper room. They passed through the city of Jerusalem and out the eastern gate north of the Temple, descended the slope of the Temple mount, crossed the Kidron brook, and ascended the Mount of Olives. They stopped for a brief time on a slope of the Mount of Olives where the Lord warned the disciples about their impending defection. Finally they arrived at the Garden of Gethsemane. Here, in a short time, Jesus was to be taken prisoner. But before that, Christ interceded with the Father. The Lord used that time of prayer to instruct His disciples on how to deal with severe temptation.

B. The Place

Gethsemane probably means "olive press" in Aramaic. Apparently that name was given to a garden or an area that included a garden on a slope of the Mount of Olives. It was called Gethsemane because the mountain was filled with olive trees. Few remain today, and those that do are old and gnarled. Some may even date back to the time of Christ. The wealthy people of Jerusalem maintained gardens on that western slope of the Mount of Olives, just east of the city. There was no room in the walled city to keep gardens because the population was dense.

The Garden of Gethsemane was a familiar place to Christ and the disciples. John 18:2 tells us they went there often. It was private—secluded from the bustle of the crowds in the city. Christ could go there to spend the night in prayer to the Father or instruct His disciples.

We don't know who owned the garden. Whoever did is another of the nameless people who served Christ toward the end of His life, such as the man who furnished Him with an animal to ride into Jerusalem and the host who provided the upper room. Commentator William Barclay said, "In a desert of hatred, there were still oases of love" (*The Gospel of Matthew,* vol. 2 [Philadelphia: Westminster, 1958], p. 384). They are nameless to us, but they are not unknown to God.

C. The People

1. Establishing the guard

When they reached the garden, somewhere near the top on the gentle slopes of the Mount of Olives, Christ told His disciples, "Sit here, while I go and pray yonder" (v. 36). Most likely, the garden was fenced or walled in, and Christ probably positioned the disciples just inside the entrance.

a) An important opportunity

The disciples knew what was about to happen. Previously Jesus had told them it was time for Him to die: "Ye know that after two days is the feast of the passover, and the Son of Man is betrayed to be crucified" (Matt. 26:2). In verse 31 He tells them, "All ye shall be offended because of me this night; for it is written, I will smite the shepherd, and the sheep of the flock shall be scattered abroad." With such a significant crisis before them, they should have taken the opportunity to pray. When Christ said He was going to pray, the disciples should have followed His lead.

Christ had a good reason for asking the disciples to stay at the entrance of the garden—He needed some seclusion. With the disciples guarding the entrance, He could be assured that His time with the Father would not be interrupted. So He set the disciples like a watch to guard Him but also to pray.

However, there is no indication that they actually prayed. They had heard Christ's prediction, but they were self-confident. They perceived themselves as invincible, confusing their good intentions for power. As a result, they didn't pray.

b) An intense objective

There is little doubt of what Christ was going to do. He told them He was going to pray. The Greek word Matthew used was *proseuchomai,* an intense word always used of praying to God, as opposed to *euchomai,* which can refer to begging or requesting something from someone. Christ was going to pour out His heart to God.

2. Instructing the leaders

Christ left all the disciples at the entrance to the garden, with the exception of Peter, James, and John, whom He took with Him. They alone of the disciples were present when Jesus raised Jairus's daughter from the dead (Mark 5:37) and when He was transfigured (Matt. 17:1). Perhaps Jesus wanted to balance their experience of His glory with a glimpse at His humiliation.

a) Christ's reason for choosing the three

Commentators through the years have debated why Jesus took Peter, James, and John with Him. We know He couldn't take all the disciples because someone had to guard the gate. And He had to leave a strong enough contingent there to discourage people from looking for Him. Furthermore, a large group of disciples would attract attention to themselves, drawing people to them instead of Christ. That explains why Christ left a large group at the entrance. But why did He take Peter, James, and John with Him to pray?

(1) Companionship

Some claim that Christ wanted those who loved Him most to be with Him to sympathize and support Him. That's a nice sentiment, and I believe it contains an element of truth since He obviously loved their companionship. But I don't believe that was His primary reason for taking them.

(2) Observation

Others believe Christ considered Peter, James, and John the weakest disciples, and therefore He couldn't let them out of His sight. But Christ gave more of Himself to those three than to any of the others. Additionally, not much could be said for the success of His discipling efforts if they were still the weakest after three years of special consideration.

(3) Instruction

I believe Jesus took them because they were the three leaders. He had a lesson that all the disciples needed to learn, but He couldn't take all eleven with Him and still maintain a guard at the gate. Jesus took Peter, James, and John because the other disciples looked to them for leadership. Whatever they learned they would communicate to the rest.

b) Christ's skill in conveying a lesson

Our Lord is always the teacher. Even though He agonized over going to the cross, He used His agony as a means for instruction. He wanted to make the most of the situation, so through His experience He taught the three disciples how to face temptation. The key to overcoming temptation is not smug self-confidence, which denies the possibility of failure, but dependence on God through intense prayer.

Jesus didn't need the disciples' help or sympathy. He never asked them to pray for Him. He didn't take them so He could keep His eye on them, otherwise He would not have left them and gone on further (v. 39). He may have gone beyond them thirty to fifty yards—Luke says He went a stone's throw (Luke 22:41). Jesus didn't want to patrol them, and He didn't need their support or sympathy. But He did want them to learn how to face a trial and pass on that lesson to others. I believe Christ also wanted them to see something of His agony that they might better understand His love.

There is a Garden of Gethsemane in all our lives. Perhaps you're experiencing agonizing trials and temptations now. The deep sorrow of a trial is something we must all pass through sooner or later. When faced with the bitter cup of trials, our social nature pushes us to reach out to others for our strength. But we often expect too much from them. Even our dearest and holiest friends, however willing their spirits might be, are still burdened by weak flesh. We need to learn to rely on God. Christ found His support in God, and He didn't ask for sympathy.

Jesus didn't need to patrol the disciples; His three-year work was complete, and He was ready to leave. The Holy Spirit would take over where He finished. Jesus took the three disciples to instruct them in how He faced a trial.

c) Christ's remedy for facing a temptation

Christ's humble acquiescence to His task provides a remarkable contrast to the confident boasting of Peter and the other disciples, who claimed they could handle the trial and wouldn't deny Christ.

(1) What sinless humanity acknowledges

Humanity is weak. Sinful fallen humanity will not acknowledge its weakness; but sinless unfallen humanity will. Jesus was conscious of the weakness of His humanity. Although He was perfect and sinless, He was human. His death proved that His humanity was weak, as death is the essence of weakness. Tears are a sign of human weakness because they're a sign of pain. Agony and suffering are a sign of human weakness. God knows no pain, agony, or suffering. But when He became a man, He experienced those things on our behalf.

(2) What sinless humanity feels

What Jesus knew about His unfallen sinlessness the disciples could not recognize in their fallen condition. When a man enters into a severe trial, he must not look to other people but to God for his strength. The disciples refused to do that. They flunked a less severe test; Christ passed the severest test in the history of humanity.

The writer of Hebrews said, "We have not an high priest [Christ] who cannot be touched with the feeling of our infirmities, but was in all points tempted like as we are, yet without sin" (4:15). When you go to the Lord with your needs, you're not talking to a high priest who doesn't know how you feel. Christ was fully human. He was "touched with the feeling of our infirmities." He experienced the weakness of humanity without committing sin. As He prepared to go to the cross, He experienced suffering, sorrow, and grief in the garden through the severe temptation of Satan. In the midst of that temptation we can sense His dependence on God. We can have victory in the midst of our trials by depending on God.

The Beginning and End of Christ's Temptation

Jesus' ministry began and ended with severe temptations. In Matthew 4, at the beginning of Christ's ministry, Satan tempts Him after He has fasted forty days in the wilderness. How many waves of temptation did Jesus face that first time? Three. In like manner Jesus faces three waves of temptation in Matthew 26:36-46. Satan attacked Him at the beginning and end of His ministry, and Jesus was victorious on both occasions.

Both temptations were personal and private solicitations to evil by Satan. We would have no insight into them if they had not been revealed to us in Scripture. But Jesus reveals both encounters to teach us profound truth. In the course of the first encounter early in His ministry, Jesus answered each temptation with Scripture. Throughout the second, Jesus responded to each temptation with prayer. When we face temptation we have two weapons at our disposal. Second Corinthians 10:4 says, "The weapons of our warfare are not carnal, but mighty through God." Those weapons are the Word of God and prayer. Ephesians 6:17-18 says to take "the sword of the Spirit, which is the word of God; praying always." If the disciples never learned anything but that, they would know enough to defeat the enemy. If we're to handle every temptation that comes our way, we do so by relying on the Word of God and the power of prayer.

II. UNFOLDING THE TEXT (vv. 37b-46)

A. Sorrow (vv. 37b-38)

1. The essence of Christ's sorrow (v. 37b)

"[Christ] began to be sorrowful and very depressed."

After having gone some distance further into the garden with Peter, James, and John, Jesus began to be sorrowful and depressed.

a) The anticipation of the cross

The Lord began to experience deep anguish. Jesus didn't go to the cross and die and then rise again without feeling anything. Every omniscient thought that anticipated the cross repulsed Him. He agonized over the reality of the cross. He despised everything connected with it—guilt, sin, death, isolation, loneliness, and estrangement from God. He didn't take it on coolly and calmly, as if He were turning a page in a book on redemptive history; it brought Him indescribable agony. His horror of the cross so repulsed Him that it's beyond our understanding.

Yet our understanding of the magnitude of the love and sacrifice of Jesus Christ is enhanced by knowing this: each time Jesus thought about the cross, He died. His omniscience allowed Him to experience His own death. Because He fully understood everything, He fully experienced His death before it ever happened. Is there any wonder that He was "a man of sorrows, and acquainted with grief" (Isa. 53:3)? The pain of the cross was always with Him, but it was in the garden that it reached its apex. His victorious endurance of that pain shows how much He loved the Father and submitted to His will and how much He loved sinners.

b) The agony of depression

Christ's anticipation of the cross brought terror, pain, and sorrow. The Greek word translated "sorrowful" (*lupeō*) means "deep sadness" in this context. According to one commentator the word translated "very depressed" (*adēmoneō*) probably means by derivation "to be away from home" (R. V. G. Tasker, *The Gospel According to St. Matthew* [Grand Rapids: Eerdmans, 1979], p. 252). Home is where comfortable things are. Home is where you belong, where your family is, where love is, where you're at ease and feel accepted. Jesus was away from home. He was isolated in conflict with hell. Such a conflict was deeply depressing. Psalm 42 is a messianic psalm that contains a description of this experience: "Deep calleth unto deep at the noise of thy waterspouts; all thy waves and thy billows are gone over me" (v. 7). Desolate loneliness and sorrow caused Christ to be deeply depressed.

Why Was Christ Depressed?

Christ was depressed not only about what had happened but also about what would happen.

1. The defection of Judas

Jesus Christ is the most fascinating human who ever lived. As the God-man, who knew only love and did only what was right, He was full of goodness, grace, mercy, and kindness. He was the trusted Friend, Lover of souls, and gracious Master adored by holy angels and guarded by seraphim. Yet He was humiliated by a wretched traitor who scorned his holy privilege.

2. The desertion of the eleven

Christ was the source of the disciples' lives. He was the resource for their needs, the comforter for every grief, and the lesson for every point of ignorance. He was their faithful Teacher, loyal Friend, Encourager, Forgiver, and Supporter. Yet He was forsaken by those whom He would never forsake. He spent three years with men who turned their backs on Him and ran to save their own lives. You would become depressed if those you loved and invested your life in forsook you.

3. The denial by Peter

Christ invested most of His time in Peter. He was not ashamed to call sinful Peter His friend. He was not ashamed to give Peter leadership of His disciples. He was not ashamed to make Peter His brother and share all His eternal riches with him. Yet Christ was to be the object of Peter's shame. Wretched, sinful Peter would deny and curse his holy Lord.

4. The rejection by Israel

The Messiah's own people rejected Him. He is the Lord of their covenant, the King of glory and grace, and the source of their hope. He came to redeem them, yet He would be rejected by them, murdered by their unbelief.

5. The injustice of men

Christ established the laws of the world. He is the God of equity, fairness, and truth. Yet He would be cheated by the petty courts whose lies would deny Him justice.

6. The cursing and mocking of the soldiers

Angels continually praise Christ. For all eternity He knew nothing but praise, adoration, and exaltation by holy creatures for His eternal perfection. Yet He would be spit on, mocked, and belittled by the profanity of men.

7. The bearing of sin

The spotless, sinless, holy Son of God would become sin. At the moment of His death He was so identified with sin that He would be called sin, even though He knew no sin. Such an experience repulsed everything in His holy nature.

8. The abandonment by God

Christ is the beloved of the Father. God said of Him, "This is my beloved Son, in whom I am well pleased" (Matt. 3:17). He is the object of eternal love. Yet He would be abandoned by the Father. In addition, Christ is a fellow of the Holy Spirit and member of the angelic association. He who communes with holy creatures, the eternally glorious Friend, would be left alone—forsaken by even the heavenly hosts.

9. The imminence of His death

As God, Jesus is immortal and eternal—He knows no death. As humans, we come into the world tasting death our whole life. Although we are fallen and sinful, still we are repulsed by death. How much more would death repulse Christ, who never knew its taste? The writer of Hebrews says, "By the grace of God, [Christ] should taste death for every man" (Heb. 2:9). He would face something an eternal being could never face, but as a man He would die for all men. Jewish scholar Alfred Edersheim said, "He disarmed Death by burying his shaft in His own Heart" (*The Life and Times of Jesus the Messiah* [Grand Rapids: Eerdmans, 1980], p. 539).

c) The attack of Satan

Christ's depression was not theater; it was reality. All that He struggled with was overwhelmingly depressing, and it amounted to a life-and-death struggle with Satan. There's no doubt in my mind that Satan was at the heart of Christ's temptation in the garden. Christ would not have experienced any struggle unless Satan was present. Certainly Christ could not have struggled with His own nature, because His nature was sinless.

(1) His method

I believe Satan tempted Christ in the garden in much the same manner as in the wilderness. The gist of Satan's temptation that first time was, "Make stones into bread, jump off the Temple, and bow down to me, and I'll give You the kingdoms of the world" (Matt. 4:1-12). Satan's ploy was to show Christ His worthiness of a better life—that He should not allow Himself to be so deprived. But that's typical of Satan. He wants us to believe we deserve more than we have (cf. Gen. 3:1-5). And I believe Satan used a similar approach in the garden: "You are the Son of God! Why are You allowing a mob to take You captive and execute You? Why is Your face in the dirt, in agony crying out to God? Why be humiliated by the desertion of eleven disciples and the betrayal of one wretched traitor? You deserve better than that! You're too worthy. You're the Son of God. Take what You're entitled to!"

(2) His motive

Satan wanted to keep Christ from the cross. In His first temptation, Satan tried to get Christ to claim His kingdom immediately, therefore bypassing the cross. Later, Satan used Peter to convey the same temptation. Jesus said to Peter, "Get thee behind me, Satan. Thou art an offense unto me; for thou savorest not the things that are of God, but those that are of men" (Matt. 16:23). Peter didn't understand God's plan. Satan brought three waves of temptation upon Christ in the garden in his attempt to stop Him from following God's plan.

2. The extent of Christ's sorrow (v. 38)

> "Then saith he [Christ] unto them [the three disciples], My soul is exceedingly sorrowful, even unto death; tarry here, and watch with me."

The Greek word translated "exceedingly sorrowful" is *perilupos,* which means "to be surrounded by sorrow." He was engulfed in sadness. Jesus said His soul—His inner being—was drowning in sorrow to the point of death. His sorrow was enough to kill Him. It is possible for a man to die from sheer anguish. The capillaries can burst. That happened to Christ. As He began to sweat in His agony, His perspiration mingled with the blood escaping through His sweat glands (Luke 22:44), a condition known as hematidrosis. Christ could have died from His anguish in the garden if God had not sent an angel to strengthen Him (v. 43). When He was crucified, Christ died quickly; the soldiers didn't have to break His legs. His anguish was so severe that death was imminent.

Christ's anguish on the cross cannot be isolated—His entire life was full of sorrow. He retreated to the Father, saying to the disciples, "Tarry here, and watch with me" (Matt. 26:38). Obviously Christ wanted them to pray with Him. They should have prayed, because He warned them about what was coming.

B. Supplication (vv. 39, 42, 44)

Verse 39 says, "He went a little further, and fell on his face, and prayed." Verse 42 says, "He went away again the second time, and prayed." Verse 44 says, "He left them, and went away again, and prayed the third time." With each wave of temptation Christ retreated into seclusion with the Father in prayer, as His grief and sorrow continued to escalate. One hint of that is Luke's reference to Christ's beginning His first prayer to the Father in a kneeling position (22:41), but Matthew says He fell on His face (26:39). Obviously Christ began by kneeling but was soon lying prostrate with His face on the ground.

1. The first supplication (v. 39)

   "He went a little further, and fell on his face, and prayed, saying, O My Father, if it be possible, let this cup pass from me; nevertheless, not as I will, but as thou wilt."

   a) The elements of Christ's prayer

      (1) His comfort in God's love

         Every time Christ prayed to God He called Him "Father" except once—when God forsook Him while He hung on the cross bearing the sin of the world (Matt. 27:46). But His prayer in Matthew 26:39 is the only record in Scripture of His referring to God as "*My* Father." He talked to God in intimate terms, something foreign to Judaism. The Jews struggled with Jesus' use of "Father" for God because they didn't refer to God as their personal Father. To them He was the Father of the nation, and there was no intimacy in that. But in verse 39 Jesus carries His intimate approach one step further and says, "O My Father." In his gospel Mark says Jesus cried "Abba, Father" (14:36). While Jesus clung to His intimacy with God, Satan tried to pry Him from the Father's will and purpose. But Jesus would not be released from that intimate relationship. He would not distrust His Father, just as He would not make bread on His own, credit Himself as the Messiah, or take on the kingdoms of the world apart from the cross (Matt. 4:1-12).

      (2) His conflict over God's plan

         After addressing God in such intimate terms, Christ said, "If it be possible, let this cup pass from me; nevertheless, not as I will, but as thou wilt" (Matt. 26:39). That is a prayer of resolution and resignation to the will of God. When Christ says, "If it be possible," He was not asking God if He had the power to let the cup pass from Him, for He knew God had that power. But He was asking if it were possible within the plan of God. Was it morally possible—was it consistent with God's plan to save sinners—to let Christ redeem sinners in another way? Christ endured unbearable anguish in the garden. In fact, just after this first prayer, Jesus began to sweat great clots of blood (Luke 22:44). The Greek word for "clots" is *thrombos,* from which the English word *thrombosis* is derived. Christ did not try to avoid God's redemptive work, but the degree of such agony led Him to ask if there were another way to accomplish it.

(3) His consumption of God's wrath

The cup Christ would drink symbolizes the experience He would endure. He would consume the cup of divine wrath to its bitter dregs. Psalm 75:8, Isaiah 51:17, Jeremiah 49:12, and other Scripture verses refer to the cup of judgment or the cup of wrath. Christ would endure the fury of God over sin, Satan, the power of death, and the guilt of iniquity. Our Lord desired to avoid that part of God's plan if there were another way.

(4) His commitment to God's will

Remember that Christ once said, "For this cause [death] came I unto this hour" (John 12:27). Therefore it is no surprise that our Lord concluded His prayer by saying, "Nevertheless, not as I will, but as thou wilt" (Matt. 26:39). Jesus once told Peter, "Thou savorest not the things that are of God, but those that are of men" (Matt. 16:23). He came into the world to do God's will, and that was His absolute and total commitment.

Christ's supplication reveals His genuine agony because we see His desire to be relieved of it. However, it was followed by His commitment to do God's will, no matter the cost. That is the way we should all face temptation, with confident prayer and commitment to the will of God. Jesus trusted God. The intensity of His struggle brought out the best in Him, because He approached it correctly. But it brought out the worst in the disciples, because they approached it incorrectly, even though their trial was infinitely less severe than His.

Focusing on the Facts

1. What caused Jesus to be a man of sorrows (see p. 26)?
2. Where is His sorrow most clearly observed? What can we learn from it (see p. 26)?
3. At what time does Christ's intercession with the Father in Matthew 26:36-46 take place (see p. 27)?
4. Where was the Garden of Gethsemane? What is the probable meaning of its name (see p. 28)?
5. Why did Jesus and His disciples often go to the Garden of Gethsemane (see p. 29)?
6. What opportunity did some of the disciples let pass when Christ left them at the entrance to the garden (see p. 29)?
7. Why did the Lord ask several of the disciples to remain near the entrance to the garden (Matt. 26:37; see pp. 29-30)?
8. What was Christ intending to do in the garden (see p. 30)?
9. Why did Jesus want Peter, James, and John to accompany Him further into the garden (see pp. 30-31)?
10. What is the key to overcoming temptation (see p. 31)?
11. Why shouldn't we rely on friends when facing a trial (see p. 32)?
12. What does sinless humanity acknowledge (see pp. 32-33)?
13. What two weapons does the believer have at his disposal when he undergoes severe temptation from Satan? Explain (see p. 34).
14. What made Christ sorrowful and depressed (Matt. 26:37)? Elaborate on several possibilities (see pp. 34-37).
15. What was Satan's method for tempting Christ in the garden (see p. 38)?
16. What was Satan's reason for tempting Christ (see p. 38)?
17. Explain the extent of Christ's sorrow (Matt. 26:38; see p. 39).
18. What physical position did Christ take as He prayed to the Father (Matt. 26:39; Luke 22:41; see p. 39)?
19. In what manner did Christ address God? Why is that significant (Matt. 26:39; see p. 40)?
20. Explain Christ's statement "If it be possible, let this cup pass from me" (Matt. 26:39; see pp. 40-41).
21. What does the cup in Matthew 26:39 symbolize (see p. 41)?

Pondering the Principles

1. What do you normally do once you realize you are in the midst of a trial? Do you turn to God for help, depend on your friends, or seek to get out of it on your own? Read 1 Corinthians 10:12-13. What does that passage teach you about the solution to a trial? Who delivers you out of a trial: yourself or God? How will the deliverance occur? Read Galatians 6:2, 5, and 1 Thessalonians 5:14. What role should other Christians play in your trial? The next time you face a trial, how will you respond?

2. In Matthew 26:39, in the midst of great sorrow, Jesus cries out to God saying, "O my Father." That reveals His great intimacy with God. How intimate are you with the Father? The depth of your relationship to Him depends on how much time you spend each day studying His Word and praying to Him. If you truly want to be closer to God, find some activities to cut out of your schedule so that you can spend more time with Him. You'll be rewarded by knowing Him better than ever before.

3. Read Matthew 26:39. How would you characterize Christ's commitment to His Father's will? How would you characterize your commitment to your Father's will? How do you respond when your desires seemingly differ from the direction God is leading? The next time that happens, will you be able to say as Christ did, "Not as I will, but as Thou wilt" (Matt. 26:39)? Memorize that verse for the next occasion.

3

The Son in Sorrow—Part 2

Outline

Introduction

Review
I. Setting the Scene (vv. 36-37*a*)
II. Unfolding the Text (vv. 37*b*-46)
   A. Sorrow (vv. 37*b*-38)
   B. Supplication (vv. 39, 42, 44)
      1. The first supplication (v. 39)
         a) The elements of Christ's prayer

Lesson
         b) The explanation of Christ's perspiration
            (1) Receiving strength from an angel
            (2) Releasing sweat mixed with blood
      2. The second supplication (v. 42)
         a) A secure companionship
         b) A strengthened commitment
      3. The third supplication (v. 44)
   C. Sleep (vv. 40, 43, 45*a*)
      1. The first instance (v. 40)
         a) The disinterest of the disciples (v. 40*a*)
            (1) The reason for their sleep
            (2) The reason for their disinterest
         b) The disappointment of Christ (v. 40*b*)
      2. The second instance (v. 43)
      3. The third instance (v. 45*a*)
   D. Strength (vv. 45*b*-46)
      1. Stating the victory (v. 45*b*)
      2. Summoning the disciples (v. 46*a*)
      3. Signifying the traitor (v. 46*b*)

Introduction

For many years I've been involved in an intensive study of the life of Christ. When I was a seminary student I went to a used bookstore and purchased old volumes on the life of Christ. I read them with eagerness and excitement, for the Lord planted a desire in my heart to know everything I could about what the Savior was like, what He said, and what He did.

Many Christians know little about Christ. All the rich, rewarding, profound, and blessed events of the Savior's life are unknown to them. I imagine there are many Christians who know the characters and details of soap operas better than the details of the life of Christ. Many Christians can tell you all about movies and movie stars, television and television personalities. Many can sing the hit songs of the last ten years; and they can tell you who sang them. Many can tell you the story line and characters in novels. Some believers know all there is to know about cars and boats. Others can give you all the batting averages for their favorite baseball teams. A couple of years ago the popularity of trivia games exploded. It is amazing to discover how much useless stuff you can crowd into your brain! We can know so much about so many things, yet know little about Jesus Christ, who is our Savior. We should love Him so much that we would not wish for any detail of His life and being to escape our knowledge.

Jesus Christ is the God-man—100 percent God and 100 percent man. In Matthew 26:39 He cries out to God for deliverance but then willingly goes to the cross. The apparent paradoxes are too profound to understand. So although we desire to know every detail about the life of Christ, we can only understand so much.

I believe Matthew 26:36-46 has been passed over by many scholars. We tend to focus on Christ's suffering on the cross to the detriment of what He suffered in the Garden of Gethsemane.

Review

I. SETTING THE SCENE (vv. 36-37*a*; see pp. 27-34)

"Then cometh Jesus with them unto a place called Gethsemane, and saith unto the disciples, Sit here, while I go and pray yonder. And he took with him Peter and the two sons of Zebedee."

II. UNFOLDING THE TEXT (vv. 37*b*-46)

A. Sorrow (vv. 37*b*-38; see pp. 34-39)

"[He] began to be sorrowful and very depressed. Then saith he unto them, My soul is exceedingly sorrowful, even unto death; tarry here, and watch with me."

B. Supplication (vv. 39, 42, 44)

In the midst of His sorrow, Jesus cried out to God three different times.

The Tempter Behind the Scenes

I believe that Christ was tempted in the garden; some people believe He wasn't. Satan's goal was to prevent Christ from going to the cross, thus preventing the resurrection. Those who disagree with that interpretation claim Satan isn't mentioned in this passage. That's true; Matthew doesn't dignify Satan. But it's obvious that Satan is behind the scenes.

While Christ and all the disciples were still in the upper room, Satan entered into Judas to accomplish his work (John 13:27). Later, as Christ instructed the remaining disciples, He said, "Hereafter I will not talk much with you; for the prince of this world cometh, and hath nothing in me" (John 14:30). Christ affirmed Satan would tempt Him but that his temptation would not succeed. As Christ approached the garden, He anticipated His impending conflict with Satan.

In Luke 22:53, as Jesus is seized by the religious leaders and soldiers, He tells them, "This is your hour, and the power of darkness." In reality, it was Satan's hour.

Jesus knew Satan was behind His arrest and eventual crucifixion, even while He was in the upper room. As Christ entered the garden, He began the most intense struggle of His life—more intense than the temptation at the beginning of His ministry. That first time there is no indication that He sweat great drops of blood. The agony of this final temptation is unequaled, as Satan attempted to keep Christ off the cross so He could not atone for sin.

As Jesus cries out to God in the midst of His temptation, we learn about His suffering, which gives us a better understanding of His love. The more we know about His love, the more thankful we ought to be. But beyond that, Christ's temptation shows those of us who would follow God's will how to meet temptation—He met temptation through prayer.

1. The first supplication (v. 39)

"He went a little further, and fell on his face, and prayed, saying, O my Father, if it be possible, let this cup pass from me; nevertheless, not as I will, but as thou wilt."

a) The elements of Christ's prayer (see pp. 40-42)

Christ was always clear about His commitment to follow God's will. In verse 39 He says, "As thou wilt," and in verse 42, "Thy will be done." Then verse 44 says, "[He] prayed the third time, saying the same words." But because the prospect of bearing sin, dying on the cross, and being separated from God was so much to bear, He asked God if there were another way to accomplish redemption. Still, Christ held fast to His willingness to follow God's plan. Make no mistake: Jesus was not trying to avoid the cross as long as it was God's will for Him to go there.

Only a few days earlier Jesus had said, "Except a grain of wheat fall into the ground and die, it abideth alone; but if it die, it bringeth forth much fruit" (John 12:24). Christ knew He had to die. In verse 27 He says, "What shall I say? Father, save me from this hour. But for this cause came I unto this hour." Christ did not ask God to save Him from death—He came into the world to die. But when faced with the pain and horror of His impending crucifixion, He asked if it were possible for God's plan to be fulfilled in another way.

Lesson

b) The explanation of Christ's perspiration

As Christ agonized in prayer over His temptation, He began to sweat. The nights are cool that time of year, so His sweat was a result of His agony. Luke 22:44 says, "His sweat was, as it were, great drops of blood." The Greek word translated "drops" is *thrombos*, which means "clots."

(1) Receiving strength from an angel

Just prior to Christ's perspiring blood, Luke 22:43 says, "There appeared an angel unto him from heaven, strengthening Him." Matthew 26:38 tells us His sorrow was so intense, that it was "unto death." Jesus might have died in the garden were it not for the strengthening from the angel. His solitary prayer intensified His struggle, as did His sorrow unto death.

(2) Releasing sweat mixed with blood

Hematidrosis, the phenomenon of sweating blood, is rare. When a person enters into extreme anguish, such as our Lord did, the resulting strain

49

can cause the dilation of the subcutaneous capillaries (those tiny blood vessels just under the
skin). As they dilate, they could burst. In the vi-
cinity of the sweat glands, blood and sweat will
then be exuded together. As Christ shed a multitude of tears (Heb. 5:7) and sweat profusely in
His agony, His capillaries burst. The clots of
blood gave a red color to beads of sweat running
down His face and dripping onto His clothing.

After that first session, having been strengthened by the
angel, He rose from prayer and returned to His disciples
(v. 40). But then He returned to prayer a second time.

2. The second supplication (v. 42)

"He went away again the second time, and prayed, saying, O my Father, if this cup may not pass away from
me except I drink it, thy will be done."

a) A secure companionship

Again Christ addressed God as *His* Father, as He con-
tinued to hold onto His intimate relationship with
God. He felt the enemy trying to pull Him away from
God's will.

b) A strengthened commitment

Then Christ changed His petition. The first time He
said, "If it be possible, let this cup pass" (v. 39). Now
He said, "If this cup may not pass away from me except I drink it [endure it], thy will be done." Again
we see that the emphasis of the temptation was to get
Christ to avoid the cross. At the cross our Lord would
experience the cup of God's wrath against sin. Although Christ asked God if the cup could pass Him
by, He knew it couldn't. So we see Him strengthened
in His commitment to do God's will.

3. The third supplication (v. 44)

"He left them, and went away again, and prayed the
third time, saying the same words."

His words may have been even more resolute. He may have said, "Since this cannot pass, Thy will be done." Instead of becoming weaker with every round, it appears He became stronger. Christ was winning the victory over the enemy.

What a beautiful picture! With strong crying and tears, great agony, and persistent supplication to God, Christ held firmly to God's will and against all that hell could bring. Satan's powers of temptation were energized to their absolute limit in his effort to keep Christ from the cross. Yet all the way through, Christ said, "Thy will be done." He was resolute in His commitment to God's will.

The Purpose of Prayer in the Midst of Temptation

There were three waves to Satan's attack, just as there were in the first temptation at the beginning of Christ's ministry (Matt. 4:1-12). Satan required three sequences to unleash his powerful temptation. Christ endured unrelenting agony as He affirmed His resolution to fulfill God's will perfectly.

Through Christ's experience we learn that "prayer is not an engine by which we overcome the unwillingness of God. God is ever ready to grant what is really good for us, when we have, by prayer, made ourselves ready to receive it" (Alfred Plummer, *An Exegetical Commentary on the Gospel According to S. Matthew* [London: Elliot Stock, 1909], p. 370). Prayer is perhaps best defined as lining up with what God wants us to do at any price, even if our lives are at stake. Satan tries to divert us from obeying God's will by appealing to our lusts. Prayer puts us in touch with God so we can tell Him, "I don't want to disobey You; strengthen me!" Prayer lines us up with God's blessing.

After the third temptation, Jesus was the victor and Satan the vanquished. The enemy of Christ's soul was gone. Christ was now in perfect harmony with the will of God, calmly prepared to move toward the cross. The key to Christ's victory was supplication—He cried out to God. And if He who is God needed to do that, how desperately we need to do the same, especially when in the midst of temptation. That is the lesson He wanted His disciples and us to learn.

C. Sleep (vv. 40, 43, 45a)

1. The first instance (v. 40)

a) The disinterest of the disciples (v. 40a)

"He cometh unto the disciples, and findeth them asleep."

The three disciples were sleeping at the moment of the greatest spiritual conflict in the history of the world. They should have been praying. That is what Christ intended for them when He left to pray on His own. In verse 41 He tells them, "Watch and pray." They had much to pray about. Were they so absolutely indifferent to the agony of Christ that they slept and couldn't stay awake to pray for their own Master? Jesus previously told them that they would be offended because of Him and be scattered abroad (v. 31). He told Peter that he would deny Him on three occasions before the cock crowed (v. 34). He even told them that He would be betrayed, offered as a sacrifice for sin, and rise again, and that it all would begin that night (John 13-16). How could they possibly sleep? They did not understand that the price of victory is vigilance.

(1) The reason for their sleep

The natural thing for the disciples to do after midnight was sleep. After all, they were weary from a busy week. Additionally, they had recently eaten a huge meal—all eleven had consumed an entire sacrificial lamb and everything that went with it, including unleavened bread and four cups of wine. Then they had completed a long walk and a hard hike up the Mount of Olives. I'm sure they felt weary. Luke adds that they also were sleepy because of sorrow (22:45). The circumstances were depressing for them—and when people become depressed, they often find escape in sleep.

(2) The reason for their disinterest

> The disciples had not come to grips with the real
> issues. When my mind is exercised over some
> spiritual conflict, I sometimes cannot sleep even
> when my body is extremely weary. The battle
> takes over. But the disciples didn't engage in the
> battle. Weakness and sinfulness caused them to
> be indifferent to the impending conflict. So they
> slept.

> We shouldn't be surprised that Peter, James, and
> John fell asleep; they also fell asleep on the mount
> of transfiguration (Luke 9:32). The intensity of
> Christ's struggle, the warning of the Lord about
> their desertion, Christ's prediction of His crucifix-
> ion, and the institution of the Lord's Supper
> should have clued them in on what was happen-
> ing.

b) The disappointment of Christ (v. 40*b*)

> "He saith unto Peter, What, could ye not watch with
> me one hour?"

> That Peter couldn't stay awake for one hour suggests
> that Christ was in prayer with the Father for that pe-
> riod of time.

2. The second instance (v. 43)

> "He came and found them asleep again; for their eyes
> were heavy."

That Jesus found them asleep *again* indicates that they
fell asleep a second time. We know the Lord awakened
them once because He told Peter, "What, could ye not
watch with me one hour? Watch and pray, that ye enter
not into temptation" (vv. 40-41). Even with that warning, they still couldn't keep alert. When He went back to
pray, they fell asleep again. Why did they fall asleep?
Their eyes were heavy. They were overpowered by their
physical impulses. While the Lord was alone in agony,
the three disciples were indifferent.

3. The third instance (v. 45*a*)

"Then cometh he to his disciples, and saith unto them,
Sleep on now, and take your rest."

The disciples were still indifferent—out of touch with
the situation. I believe it is best to translate the phrase
"sleep on now, and take your rest" as a question. The
New International Version translates it that way. Jesus
was asking them a pensive, painful question: "Are you
still sleeping and taking your rest?" They were unaware
of the nature of the spiritual battle.

Indifferent to the needs of Christ and the power of the enemy, the disciples were about to be totally overwhelmed by
the circumstances and forsake Christ (v. 56). They would
never pass the temptation. They would fall into sin and reject Christ. At the moment of crisis, they would run away.
They weren't ready. Our Lord's lesson is clear: victory be-
longs to those who are alert in all spiritual battles—those
who have recognized their weaknesses. The disciples were
fools, believing they would never be offended because of
Christ and claiming they were prepared to go to prison or
die before denying Him. They put too much stock in their
good intentions. Victory isn't won by those who sleep
when the battle is imminent but by those who are vigilant.
It's a tragedy to see spiritual self-confidence, for it betrays a
state of unpreparedness.

D. Strength (vv. 45*b*-46)

1. Stating the victory (v. 45*b*)

"Behold, the hour is at hand, and the Son of man is betrayed into the hands of sinners."

When Christ made that statement, I believe He saw the
Roman soldiers and Jewish leaders, accompanied by Judas, carrying their torches and swords and moving up
the Mount of Olives. The sinless Son of God was about
to be arrested by sinners. As they came, the disciples
were sleeping. But Christ was victorious. He had defeated the hosts of hell. He stood victorious, covered with
bloody sweat, courageously prepared to face the cross.

While He had been conquering the enemy in the strength of His Father, the disciples had slept.

2. Summoning the disciples (v. 46*a*)

"Rise, let us be going."

Christ was not encouraging the disciples to flee with Him. The Greek word translated "going" is a military term meaning "to go forward," as in going to meet an advancing enemy. Jesus was strengthened in His temptation. He was victorious. Now He was ready to confront His captors—they didn't have to find Him.

As He approached them He said, "Whom seek ye? They answered him, Jesus, of Nazareth. Jesus saith unto them, I am he" (John 18:4-5). When He said that, they all fell to the ground (v. 6). Christ exemplifies great courage. Satan tempted Jesus to disbelieve that God would raise Him from the dead. But He committed Himself to the One who is able to raise the dead. So with confidence He moved resolutely toward His captors. He saw beyond the cross to the joy that was set before Him (Heb. 12:2). He willingly endured the cross.

Scripture doesn't say we're to run from the devil. It says, "*Resist* the devil, and he will flee from you" (James 4:7, emphasis added). We're to stand our ground. We resist him in the strength of prayer and the Word of God, as Christ demonstrated in both of His temptations. We can defeat the enemy with the two-edged sword of the Word and prayer.

3. Signifying the traitor (v. 46*b*)

"Behold, he is at hand that doth betray me."

When Christ said, "The Son of man is betrayed into the hands of sinners" (v. 45), He was referring to all those who would be responsible for His execution. But the one leading the parade of sinners was Judas. The Greek word translated "betray" means "deliver." Judas was the one who delivered Christ into the hands of sinners. But Christ went on to meet him victoriously.

E. Sequence (v. 41)

After His first session of prayer, Jesus said to Peter, "What, could ye not watch with me one hour?" (v. 40). Then He gave the principle I believe He was intending to teach them.

1. Establishing the principle for victory (v. 41*a*)

"Watch and pray, that ye enter not into temptation."

Christ was telling them to stay alert and stay in prayer. He was encouraging them to discern when they were in the midst of spiritual warfare and turn to God. They were not to let their self-confidence lull them to sleep. The way to avoid temptation is to stay alert to it—to be aware of Satan's devices (2 Cor. 2:11)—and then to go to the Father in prayer.

Peter learned that principle. In 2 Peter 2:9 he says, "The Lord knoweth how to deliver the godly out of temptations." You go to God for deliverance. The scout for the army doesn't engage in battle with the enemy once he finds them; that would be idiotic. Instead, he returns to tell the commander what he's learned, and then the commander leads the troops into battle. No Christian can be victorious in fighting Satan by himself; he must report to the Commander. Jesus Himself sought out our heavenly Father for divine strength.

In Matthew 6:13 Jesus teaches us to pray, "Lead us not into temptation, but deliver us from evil." We can accomplish that through the Lord only; we can't do it on our own. The disciples thought they could. But they denied and forsook Christ.

2. Explaining the principle for victory (v. 41*b*)

"The spirit indeed is willing, but the flesh is weak."

Every believer has a problem that Christ didn't have. His perfection allowed Him to act and respond without sin in every occasion of temptation. But we have a unique problem: a willing spirit but weak flesh. Regenerated people love God and desire to do what is right. No doubt Peter, James, and John loved the Savior and wanted to do what was right. I'm sure the other eight disciples also wanted to do what was right, but they were weak.

a) Peter's explanation

I'm sure Peter suffered greatly over his denial, because that was the last thing he wanted to do (Matt. 26:33, 35). In 1 Peter 5:8 he says, "Be sober, be vigilant, because your adversary, the devil, like a roaring lion walketh about, seeking whom he may devour." Peter learned that lesson right in the Garden of Gethsemane. He could teach that with conviction, because Satan devoured all the disciples on the night the Lord needed them the most. They didn't want to abandon the Lord, but they did.

b) Paul's explanation

How can you be victorious? The apostle Paul gives us the answer in Galatians 5:16: "Walk in the Spirit, and ye shall not fulfill the lust of the flesh." Victory results when a believer walks in obedience to the Holy Spirit, fills himself with the Word of God, and yields his life to God's Spirit.

Conclusion

A. The Sequence for Disaster

The sequence for disaster in the midst of temptation is confidence, sleep, temptation, sin, disaster. The confident believer claims he can handle any temptation. He maintains that he doesn't need to pray. He says he will never deny the Lord. He is sure he will remain faithful. He firmly believes he will always be strong enough to be victorious. Sleep then follows confidence. After all, what would he need to be vigilant about? The confident believer doesn't see a need to guard what he sees, reads, hears, and thinks.

Sleep then leads to temptation and from that to sin and disaster. That's the way the disciples lived.

B. The Sequence for Victory

We see a different pattern in Jesus' life. Instead of being confident He was humble. Jesus recognized the weakness of His humanness, even though He was sinless. So, while the disciples were claiming confidently that they would never fail Christ, Jesus turned to God for strength. The disciples' confidence led to sleep, whereas Christ's humility led to prayer. But after the temptation came Christ's obedience to the will of God. And that was followed by victory. You have a choice. You can either be self-confident and end up in disaster or you can be humble, fall on your knees before God in prayer for strength, and then commit yourself to God's will in the midst of temptation. The latter is the only way to victory.

Focusing on the Facts

1. Why do many Christians know so little about the life of Christ (see p. 46)?
2. How can we know Jesus was being tempted by Satan in the Garden of Gethsemane (see pp. 47-48)?
3. What happened to Christ in the midst of His agony (Luke 22:44)? Explain how that could have happened (see pp. 49-50).
4. According to Matthew 26:42, in what way did Christ change His petition to God (see p. 50)?
5. Give a definition of prayer as it relates to temptation (see p. 51).
6. Why should the disciples have been praying instead of sleeping? What didn't they understand (see p. 52)?
7. Why were the disciples sleeping? What were they indifferent to (see pp. 52-53)?
8. How often did the three disciples fall asleep (see pp. 53-54)?
9. Explain the significance of Christ's statement to the disciples, "Rise, let us be going" (Matt. 26:46; see p. 55).
10. How does a believer effectively resist the devil (see p. 55)?
11. According to Matthew 26:41, what is the principle for victory? Explain it (see p. 56).

12. In facing temptation, what problem do believers have that Christ didn't have (see pp. 56-57)?
13. What is the sequence for disaster? What is the sequence for victory (see pp. 57-58)?

Pondering the Principles

1. How much do you know about Christ? Are there earthly things you know more about? What are they? How many of them warrant more attention from you than the life of Christ? If you want to know more about the life of Christ, you can begin a study of His life in the gospels. You will need to obtain a harmony of the gospels to capture the chronological flow of His life. You also may want to obtain a book on His life; there are many fine ones available, such as *The Life and Times of Jesus the Messiah*, by Alfred Edersheim. Commit yourself to studying about Him each day.

2. Are you like the disciples, indifferent to the spiritual battles taking place around you? Or have you taken heed to Christ's warning to watch and pray, knowing that vigilance will pay off in victory? Be specific in your analysis. How can you turn your indifference into victory? What things can you do to become more alert to temptation? How often do you ask God to reveal your weaknesses? And when you do enter a time of temptation, do you seek to get out of it yourself, or do you turn to God? Ask God to show you the battles occurring around you. Be aware of how Satan operates (2 Cor. 2:11). Dig into His Word so you might be better able to recognize temptation. Finally, develop a richer prayer life. Get to know your Father in heaven by spending more time with Him.

4
The Traitor's Kiss—Part 1

Outline

Introduction

Lesson
I. The Attack of the Crowd (v. 47)
   A. Reviewing the Scene
   B. Identifying the Participants
      1. Judas
         a) The mystery of his betrayal
         b) The method of his betrayal
         c) The motivation of his betrayal
         d) The mobilization of his betrayal
            (1) Gaining Pilate's permission
            (2) Gaining police protection
      2. The multitude
         a) Their identity
            (1) Jewish leaders
            (2) Roman soldiers
            (3) Temple police
         b) Their torches
         c) Their weapons
            (1) Swords
            (2) Clubs
II. The Kiss of the Traitor (vv. 48-50*a*)
   A. The Sign of the Betrayal (v. 48)
      1. Paying homage
      2. Feigning innocence
      3. Selling Christ

B. The Intensity of Judas (v. 49)

C. The Response of Christ (v. 50*a*)

Conclusion

Introduction

Matthew 26:47-56 generates a great deal of emotion in me. I feel both anger and love, a desire for revenge, yet complete trust in the plan of God. I feel that way because this passage relates to us the betrayal and arrest of Jesus Christ. I trust that my anger is holy indignation at the way the Son of God was treated. The kiss of Judas is a despicable and repulsive act. It is demeaning, unfair, and unjust. Yet I also find much comfort in the response of Christ, who remained perfectly at peace with the unfolding of God's redemptive plan.

If there is a more ugly or repulsive word in the English language than the word *traitor*, it has to be the name *Judas.* Our text brings us face-to-face with the worst traitor of all. The Man of Sorrows, who was so intimately acquainted with grief, braced Himself for another painful experience. He would be betrayed by one of His disciples and then arrested and executed on a cross.

Matthew 26:47-56 is a narrative passage, and as we go through it, we find ourselves drawn into the tragedy as well as the triumph of its scenario. As I meditated on how to approach this passage, I thought it would be best to identify the different participants in the scene. So we will examine the attack of the crowd, the kiss of the traitor, the defeat of the disciples, and the triumph of the Savior.

Lesson

I. THE ATTACK OF THE CROWD (v. 47)

"While he yet spoke, lo, Judas, one of the twelve, came, and with him a great multitude with swords and clubs, from the chief priests and elders of the people."

A. Reviewing the Scene

Matthew, Mark, and Luke all say that while Jesus was speaking, the mob arrived (Mark 14:43; Luke 22:47). What was Christ saying? Let's look at the setting.

Six days previous, Jesus arrived in Bethany at the home of Mary, Martha, and Lazarus. Jesus had recently raised Lazarus from the dead (John 11:44). The next day, Sunday, great crowds went to Bethany to see Him and hear Him teach. On Monday He entered the city of Jerusalem, and the people proclaimed Him as Messiah. On Tuesday He cleansed the Temple and threw the money-changers, buyers, and sellers out of the Temple courtyard. On Wednesday He taught the multitudes in the Temple. When confronted by the religious leaders, He condemned them for their hypocrisy (Matthew 23). Late Wednesday afternoon He left the Temple with His disciples, climbed the Mount of Olives, and taught them about His second coming (Matt. 24-25). On Thursday the Lord sent Peter and John to prepare for the Passover feast. That evening after sunset, He celebrated the Passover with all the disciples in an upper room in the house of an unnamed follower. It was there that He washed the disciples' feet, taught them many things (John 13-16), prayed for them (John 17), and instituted the Lord's Table, or Communion. Near midnight He left the upper room and the city with the disciples. They ascended the Mount of Olives, and He warned them of the impending trial they would face and their ultimate defection. Although they denied that such a thing could happen, it nonetheless came to pass.

As we approach Matthew 26:47, it is around midnight on Thursday. Jesus and the eleven disciples (Judas having been dismissed during the Passover meal) reached a place to which they often went: the Garden of Gethsemane. As they entered the gate of the garden, Jesus told eight of the disciples to guard the entrance. He continued with Peter, James, and John to a more secluded place in the garden. Then Jesus left the three and went a short distance away so that He might be alone to pray. It is then that Satan hurled three great waves of temptation at Him to divert Jesus from dying on the cross for the sins of the world.

Now the prayer time was over. Sadly, the disciples slept instead of praying. After Christ's third session of prayer was complete, He returned to the disciples and said, "Behold, the hour is at hand, and the Son of man is betrayed into the hands of sinners. Rise, let us be going; behold, he is at hand that doth betray me" (Matt. 26:45-46). As He spoke, the crowd approached, climbing up the Mount of Olives. That sets the scene of the phrase "while he yet spoke" in verse 47.

B. Identifying the Participants

1. Judas

   a) The mystery of his betrayal

   In verse 47 Matthew says, "Lo, Judas, one of the twelve, came." The phrase "one of the twelve" was a common designation for Judas. Mark 14:10 calls him, "Judas Iscariot, one of the twelve." In verse 20 Jesus says, "It is one of the twelve, that dippeth with me in the dish." Verse 43 says, "Immediately, while he yet spoke, cometh Judas, one of the twelve." Luke 22:3 and 47 also refer to him as one of the twelve.

   That designation, rather than carrying just disdain and repulsiveness, is surrounded with a profound mystery. It's almost too hard to believe that the man who betrayed Jesus was actually one of the twelve. Judas knew Christ more intimately than anyone other than the rest of the disciples, yet he still betrayed Him. It's inconceivable. "One of the twelve" is primarily a statement of shock.

   b) The method of his betrayal

   Judas arrived with the multitude early Friday morning, bringing his plot to a climax. He had left the presence of the disciples earlier Thursday night (John 13:30), before Jesus had instituted the Lord's Table. He then concluded his agreement with the Jewish leaders, having previously made a contract with them, saying, "What will ye give me, and I will deliver Him unto you?" (Matt. 26:15). So Judas went to the leaders that night and told them it was the right moment, and that they must act quickly to take advantage of Jesus' separation from the crowds.

c) The motivation of his betrayal

Judas was motivated by greed. He was also possessed by Satan at that time (John 13:27), and thus no longer in control of his behavior. He was compelled to rally the Jewish leaders and Roman soldiers to capture Christ. Judas wanted compensation for what he believed were wasted years of poverty. He followed a Messiah who was not going to bring about an earthly kingdom or exalt him to the glory he had expected.

d) The mobilization of his betrayal

(1) Gaining Pilate's permission

After Judas left the upper room on Thursday night, he was a part of frantic activity. First, he reported immediately to the Jewish leaders. They had to get permission from the Romans to arrest Jesus. Most likely they met with Pilate himself. Pilate was in Jerusalem at that time, although as governor his headquarters were located in Caesarea. Matthew 27:62-63 says, "The next day, that followed the day of the preparation, the chief priests and Pharisees came together unto Pilate, saying, Sir, we remember that that deceiver said, while he was yet alive, After three days I will rise again." There the leaders identified Christ as the deceiver, which indicates they must have had some prior conversation with Pilate about Jesus to identify Him in such a manner.

To obtain permission from Pilate to arrest Jesus, the Jewish leaders had to convince him that Jesus was a potential insurrectionist and terrorist—that He was planning to lead an insurrection against Rome. The Romans were not anxious for another one; they had just quelled one not long before.

Mark 15:7 says, "There was one named Barabbas, who lay bound with them that had made insurrection with him, who had committed murder in the insurrection." Barabbas had been the leader of a terrorist revolt against Rome. The leaders wanted Rome to see Jesus as a potential Barabbas, so they said whatever they had to to convince Pilate that Jesus was a threat.

(2) Gaining police protection

On that pretense, the Roman soldiers joined the Jewish leaders as Judas led the way to the Garden of Gethsemane to take Christ captive. They may have checked the upper room first to see if Jesus and His disciples were still there. When they found He wasn't, Judas knew where He'd be. That made the capture easier, because the garden was outside the city. It was still dark, and they could proceed to the garden without being disruptive.

Roman soldiers were present throughout the city. Extra troops were necessary to keep peace during the Passover season, so an entourage of Roman soldiers marching through the city wasn't unusual. It also wouldn't be unusual for a group of Jewish leaders to pass through the streets since Passover was one of the highest and holiest of religious celebrations. If the soldiers and leaders convened outside the gate, the populace would not have been aware of what was happening.

The right moment had come. Satan knew it and entered into Judas to see the plan to its conclusion. Judas convinced the religious leaders that it was the perfect opportunity, and they in turn convinced the Romans. But for all their secret planning, they were falling in line with the plan of God. All they were doing had been decided previously "by the determinant counsel and foreknowledge of God" (Acts 2:23).

2. The multitude

a) Their identity

Matthew 26:47 tells us that a great multitude accompanied Judas on his God-ordained mission. We have discussed that multitude already to some degree, but let's examine it more specifically.

(1) Jewish leaders

Matthew 26:47 identifies one part of the multitude: "chief priests and elders of the people." The chief priests led the religious activity of Israel; the elders were members of the Sanhedrin, the ruling body of Israel. It is important to remember that the Jewish leaders were behind the arrest of Christ. By no means can we conclude that all Jewish people in the nation wanted Him arrested—they were victimized and misled by their leadership. John 18:3 says Judas "received a band of men and officers from the chief priests and Pharisees." Present were the Sadducees, who were the chief priests, the Pharisees, who for the most part made up the regular priesthood, and members of the Sanhedrin. The high priest may also have been with them. John 18:10 says the servant of the high priest was with the crowd. He was an important person, serving as an assistant to the high priest, who held the highest religious office in the land.

(2) Roman soldiers

John 18:3 says there was a "band of men and officers." The Greek word translated "band" is *speira*, which refers to a cohort of soldiers. A *speira* was specifically one-tenth of a legion in the Roman army. A legion contained six thousand men, so one-tenth of that is six hundred men. The Roman soldiers were there because they were under the impression that Jesus was an insurrectionist like Barabbas. According to verse 12 the band of

Roman soldiers was commanded by a "captain" (Gk., *chiliarch*), an officer with a rank higher than what we know as a colonel. His troops were stationed at Fort Antonia, which was located just north of the Temple ground.

(3) Temple police

Luke 22:52 adds one more group to the throng: the "captains of the temple." They were the Temple police.

b) Their torches

John 18:3 says the Roman soldiers and Jewish leaders came with "lanterns and torches." But they did not necessarily need them just to see their way in the dark. Passover occurred in the middle of the month, and there would have been a full moon at that time. A full moon in that part of the world is bright. I believe they carried lanterns and torches because they assumed they would have to hunt Jesus down and drag Him out of hiding.

c) Their weapons

Matthew 26:47 tells us they also carried "swords and clubs."

(1) Swords

The Greek word translated "sword" is *machaira*. It was a short sword—a dagger—the kind carried by a Roman soldier. When Paul outlines the armor of the Christian in Ephesians 6, he uses *machaira* in reference to the "sword of the Spirit" (v. 17). Soldiers also carried a large broad sword when they entered into armed conflict with another army. But they would carry the more deft weapon on an occasion like this one, when they were going to make an arrest.

(2) Clubs

The crowd also came carrying clubs (Gk., *zula*). These clubs were like the nightsticks that policemen carry. It was a normal weapon of the Temple police. Both the Jews and Romans were armed.

What a shocking scene! Instead of welcoming, embracing, and worshiping the long-awaited Messiah, the Jewish leaders sent a group of soldiers and Temple police to arrest Him.

Characteristics of a Wicked World

The world's wickedness has never been more obvious than in its treatment of Jesus Christ. If you don't believe the world is wicked, then ask yourself how it can reject the most pure and lovely person who ever walked on the face of the earth.

1. The world is unjust

Did the Jewish leaders have the right to execute Jesus Christ? What crime had He committed? Pilate said, "I find in him no fault at all" (John 18:38). Here was a man educated in jurisprudence and law. He knew Christ had done nothing wrong.

2. The world is mindless

What did the Roman soldiers have against Jesus Christ? Nothing. Many of the priests had nothing against Christ. They were simply following the high priest and the chief priests, who were intimidated by Christ. The priests were supposed to care for the people of Israel, and Jesus did the same. He healed their diseases, restored them to spiritual life, and taught them divine truth. The priests had nothing against Him, but they were mindless. They were caught up in the mood of the mob. One or two perverted leaders can stir up an entire populace. The crowd was as mindless as those who followed Hitler or any other evil dictator. They sold themselves to emotion. They hated One they didn't know and despised what they couldn't understand. They were hirelings of the high priest, bribed to preserve a peace they imagined could not exist unless Christ was executed.

Today the world is much the same. There are people across our nation who reject Jesus Christ just as mindlessly. All who would reject Christ had better consider His claims before they reject Him. So many people won't receive Jesus Christ because they don't believe any of His claims. My response is: "You must have conducted an in-depth study into the life of Christ to come to such a conclusion." Many people believe the Bible isn't true, yet most would confess they have never read it. Today many people follow the mood of the mob—if their friends or society rejects Christ, so will they. But that response is as mindless as that of the Roman soldiers and the priests. My message to unbelievers is, Don't be mindless. Don't become a victim of someone else's bitterness. Don't reject the Son of God because someone else did.

3. The world is cowardly

Hundreds of men carrying swords, clubs, and torches went to arrest one Galilean. A guilty conscience will make a coward out of anyone. Wicked people fear that they might receive what they know they deserve. They don't want to hear the truth. They shun honest confrontation. Nowhere do we read that even one of them went to Jesus to determine if He was an insurrectionist or if He indeed was the Messiah, the Son of God. These cowards arrived in great numbers at night, fearing exposure. Cowards are bold only when the odds are overwhelmingly in their favor.

If you can isolate an unbeliever from his support group, he instantly becomes vulnerable. He finds protection with other unbelievers. If he has surrounded himself with enough people who think and live as he does, he is comfortable in his evil. He won't confront truth in a one-on-one situation; he will hide in the cowardliness of the mob.

4. The world is profane

The world has absolutely no reverence for what is sacred. Every time I hear the name of Jesus uttered as a curse, I shudder. Every time God or Christ is mocked, every time God's Word and will is disdained, and every time Christ is rejected, that is akin to the profanity exhibited in the garden. There the world profaned the most sacred thing in the universe: God in human flesh. What blatant impiety! What unbelievable sacrilege was

70

committed when murderous, sinful hands seized the holy Lord. Jesus said, "The Son of man is betrayed into the hands of sinners" (Matt. 26:45). It is no different today. Our profane, unholy world mocks Christ and treats Him with indignity and disrespect.

The world is unjust, mindless, cowardly, and profane. All elements of evil present at the arrest in the garden have not since passed. The world is still the same.

II. THE KISS OF THE TRAITOR (vv. 48-50a)

A. The Sign of the Betrayal (v. 48)

"He that betrayed him gave them a sign, saying, Whomsoever I shall kiss, that same is he; hold Him fast."

A signal was necessary. It was dark. There was nothing external about Christ that distinguished Him from any other human being. They needed a sign so they wouldn't grab the wrong person. Perhaps they believed the disciples might try to identify an imposter as Christ. That Judas chose a kiss to signal the betrayal is an illustration of his perverted thinking.

1. Paying homage

A kiss was a mark of homage, such as that offered by a pupil to a beloved teacher as a sign of respect and love. But it could be given only when the teacher offered it first. It was considered brash to offer a kiss to a teacher unless it had been invited by the teacher's initial embrace. A kiss was a sign of affection.

Inferiors kissed the back of their superior's hand. If they were above the level of a servant, they could kiss the palm. Slaves often kissed the feet. Those who sought pardon from an angry monarch would also kiss the feet. Kissing the hem of a superior's garment was an expression of great reverence. But a kiss on the cheek was a sign of affection, love, and intimacy. Thus the kiss of Judas was despicable.

2. Feigning innocence

Judas could have kissed Christ's hand or the hem of His garment, but he feigned affection for Christ, not only to provide a sign but also to attempt to deceive Christ and the disciples. "I shall kiss" (Gk., *phileō*) is the future tense of *phileō*, which means "to show affection." Judas was feigning innocence, a weak attempt on his part to conceal his character and treachery. It would be bad enough to betray a friend, but inconceivably, Judas sold out the very Son of God! The delusion of thinking that he could deceive Him added to his sin beyond description. Judas fulfills the words of Proverbs 27:6: "The kisses of an enemy are deceitful." Integral to an enemy's deceit is an exaggeration of his friendship.

3. Selling Christ

The hatred of the priests, the raucous screams of the crowds, the pitiful cowardice of Pilate, and the brutality of the soldiers—Jesus suffered through it all with a quiet spirit. But I can't imagine what He felt in His heart as Judas kissed Him. It is inconceivable that a man could return such treachery for divine love.

An Old Testament parallel to Judas's treachery is in Ezekiel 13:19, where God says, "Will ye pollute me among my people for handfuls of barley and for pieces of bread?" His betrayal is reminiscent of Amos 2:6, where the Lord says, "They sold the righteous for silver, and the poor for a pair of shoes." Only in Christ's case, He was sold by Judas for thirty pieces of silver and betrayed with a kiss.

Judas is no less guilty because Jesus accomplished redemption—that didn't mitigate his guilt; it merely overrode his evil. So Judas concluded his betrayal by telling the leaders to seize Christ immediately after he kissed Him.

B. The Intensity of Judas (v. 49)

"Forthwith he came to Jesus, and said, Hail, master; and kissed him."

As soon as Jesus came into view, Judas said, "Hail, master." Then he kissed him. The Greek word translated "kissed" is *kataphilēsō*. It is *philēsō* intensified. Judas fervently embraced and kissed Jesus. *Kataphilēsō* is used of a groom kissing his new bride. It is also used of the woman who profusely kissed the Savior's feet (Luke 7:38).

In the midst of Judas's kisses Jesus said, "Judas, betrayest thou the Son of man with a kiss?" (Luke 22:48). Judas profaned a holy act. Psalm 2:12 says, "Kiss the Son." The Son desires a holy kiss, not a profane one. Judas acted like a person who was grieving. Perhaps he hoped to make Jesus and the disciples believe he had come to warn Christ. So he separated himself from the crowd and feigned sorrow and love.

C. The Response of Christ (v. 50*a*)

"Jesus said unto him, Friend, why art thou come?"

The best translation of the Greek word *hetairos* is not "friend" but "fellow." Jesus did not address Judas as a friend at this point. The word *philos* was reserved for a friend. It is used in John 15:15 when Jesus tells His disciples, "I have called you friends." By that time, Judas had left the upper room. Judas was not a friend but a companion in the sense of still being associated with Christ.

The correct order in the Greek text for what Jesus tells Judas is: "on what you are here." The best translation of that is: "get on with what you are here to do." How could He say that? He had just finished a serious time of prayer with His Father, and He had resolved His commitment. So He endured the betrayer's kisses and said, "Get this over with." That was the farewell of Jesus to the son of perdition. As Judas lives for eternity in hell, he must still have these words ringing in his ears: "Betrayest thou the Son of man with a kiss?" (Luke 22:48).

The Characteristics of a False Disciple

Judas was a false disciple. I can't imagine anything more wicked than that. What are the marks of a false disciple, as exemplified by Judas?

1. Greed

Judas loved money. He lived for today—he wanted glory and success. He had a greater regard for things than he did for God. He had a greater desire for self than He did for Christ. Typically, false disciples will follow Jesus to get what they want. But when Jesus doesn't deliver and puts demands on them that they didn't expect, they leave. And they may try to get all they can before they leave. They're like the seed that springs up quickly but then withers and dies when the sun comes out (Matt. 13:6). Or they are like the seed that falls among the thorns and is choked out (Matt. 13:7)—they follow Christ for a while but eventually sell Him out for their selfish desires, such as money, prestige, and power. False disciples love darkness. They love what's in the world, and they'll sell the Savior for it, as Esau sold his birthright for a pot of stew (Gen. 25:33-34).

2. Deceit

False disciples masquerade their true character in an attempt to delude others. They pretend to love the Lord. Judas was obviously successful because none of the disciples suspected him. When Jesus revealed that one of them would betray Him, each one asked, "Is it I?" (Matt. 26:22). False disciples are so deceitful that our Lord said believers can't determine for sure who's real and who isn't (Matt. 13:29).

3. Hypocrisy

Judas kissed Christ to kill Him. He paid homage on the outside, but he hated on the inside.

Judas is no solitary monster. People like him exist in every age—even today. They pretend to love Christ but in reality are greedy, deceitful, and hypocritical. They follow Christ for what they might receive—a salved conscience, peace of mind, reputation, self-satisfaction, or improved profits in business. If the truth were known, they would sell Christ if they could see greater gain somewhere else.

Conclusion

One day we will find ourselves in our own Garden of Gethsemane. Will we stand with the crowd? Will we betray Christ like Judas? Will we run away with the disciples? Or will we stand beside the triumphant Savior? Where will you stand? If you do not know the Lord Jesus Christ as your Savior, if you're not bowing at His feet and worshiping Him, He calls you to do so today.

Focusing on the Facts

1. Describe the setting of the betrayal of Christ (see pp. 63-64).
2. What is significant about the phrase "one of the twelve" as it applies to Judas (see p. 64)?
3. What motivated Judas to betray Christ (see p. 65)?
4. What did the Jewish leaders have to do before they could convince Pilate to give them permission to arrest Jesus (see pp. 65-66)?
5. Identify the Jewish leaders who came to arrest Jesus (see p. 67).
6. How many Roman soldiers assisted with the arrest of Jesus (see p. 67)?
7. What other possible reason besides seeing at night could the mob have had for carrying torches and lanterns (see p. 68)?
8. Describe the swords and clubs that the mob carried (see pp. 68-69).
9. Name some characteristics of this wicked world. Explain each one (see pp. 69-71).
10. Why was a signal necessary to identify Christ (see p. 71)?
11. What are some of the various things kissing symbolized in the culture of Jesus' day (see p. 71)?
12. What was Judas attempting to show by kissing Jesus on the cheek (see p. 72)?
13. Cite two Old Testament parallels to Judas's treachery (see p. 72).
14. In what way did Judas kiss Christ (see p. 73)?

15. What is significant about the way Jesus addressed Judas (Matt. 26:50; see p. 73)?
16. What are the characteristics of a false disciple (see p. 74)?

Pondering the Principles

1. In spite of all the secret plotting of Judas and the religious leaders, Jesus was delivered to them by "the determinate counsel and foreknowledge of God" (Acts 2:23). The phrase "determinate counsel" refers to God's will, and the word "foreknowledge" to God's ordained plan. Knowing that, how would you interpret Acts 2:23? Now look at the rest of the verse: "Ye have taken, and by wicked hands have crucified and slain." How does that relate to the first half of the verse? What is your responsibility to God's will and plan?

2. Review the section on the characteristics of a wicked world. As believers we remain sinful. Which of the characteristics would you say you exhibit more than you should? Why? Make it your goal this week to isolate one of them. Confess that sin to God and repent of it by asking God to help you become obedient to Him in that area. Make a personal study of that area in Scripture your first step toward consistent obedience.

3. A false disciple is characterized by greed, deceit, and hypocrisy. A true disciple, while wanting to obey Christ always, may still fall into bad habits and exhibit some or all of those characteristics to some degree. Which one is most characteristic of you? As in the previous question, confess your sin to God and repent of it.

5
The Traitor's Kiss—Part 2

Outline

Review
I. The Attack of the Crowd (v. 47)
II. The Kiss of the Traitor (vv. 48-50a)

Lesson
III. The Defeat of the Disciples (vv. 50b-54, 56a)
    A. The Action of the Multitudes (v. 50b)
    B. The Arrogance of Peter (v. 51)
    C. The Approach of Christ (vv. 52-54, 56)
        1. The declaration of non-violence (v. 52a)
           a) The principle
           b) The practice
        2. The reasons for non-violence (vv. 52b-54, 56a)
           a) Violence is fatal (v. 52b)
              (1) Genesis 9:6
              (2) Romans 13:4
           b) Violence is foolish (v. 53)
           c) Violence undermines the plan of God (vv. 54, 56a)
    D. The Abandonment of the Disciples (v. 56b)
IV. The Triumph of the Savior (v. 55)
    A. In His Confrontation with the Crowd
        1. He established His power (John 18:4-8)
        2. He exposed their evil (Matthew 26:55)
    B. In His Confrontation with Judas
    C. In His Confrontation with Peter

Conclusion

The events traditionally known as the passion of our Lord Jesus Christ are those encompassing His death on the cross. We are presently studying two of those particular events: the betrayal and arrest of Christ in Matthew 26:47-56. In them we see the climax of Judas's plot to acquire compensation for what he believed were wasted years in following One who didn't turn out to be the earthly king he hoped for.

Bethlehem gave the world its most honorable citizen, Jesus Christ. A small town twenty-three miles south of Jerusalem named Kerioth gave the world its most despicable character, Judas Iscariot. Jesus confronted Judas about the betrayal to come Thursday night while He was celebrating the Passover with all His disciples. After sending Judas away to carry out his plan, Jesus instituted the Lord's Supper, taught the remaining eleven, and prayed to the Father on their behalf. Then He departed with the eleven to the Garden of Gethsemane, located on the Mount of Olives. There the Lord entered into prayer and staved off three waves of Satan's temptations. Jesus was strengthened by an angel and persisted in His commitment to go to the cross. After His third time of prayer the Lord woke up the sleeping disciples to inform them that the time of His betrayal was at hand. In the distance He could see the torches and lanterns carried by the mob led by Judas coming to arrest Him.

Perhaps the best way to understand Matthew 26:47-56 is to look at the participants. We will study the attack of the mob, the kiss of the traitor, the defection of the disciples, and the triumph of the Savior.

I. THE ATTACK OF THE CROWD (v. 47; see pp. 62-71)

"While he yet spoke, lo, Judas, one of the twelve, came, and with him a great multitude with swords and clubs, from the chief priests and elders of the people."

The chief priests and elders engineered the plot to arrest Jesus after Judas sold out. But they weren't about to go alone. They tried that once before: the Temple police went to capture Jesus and came back empty-handed (John 7:32, 45). So they enlisted the help of the Romans, convincing them that Jesus posed a clear threat to Roman security.

That scene is a good illustration of the wickedness of a Christ-rejecting world. Today many people will attack Christ and reject Him as their Lord and God. They see Him as a threat to their comfortable life-styles.

II. THE KISS OF THE TRAITOR (vv. 48-50*a*; see pp. 71-75)

"He that betrayed him gave them a sign, saying, Whomsoever I shall kiss, that same is he; hold him fast. And forthwith he came to Jesus, and said, Hail, master; and kissed him. And Jesus said unto him, Friend, why art thou come? [Do what you have come to do.]"

Judas is the epitome of lost opportunity. No one has ever had a greater opportunity to be saved. But Judas loved money—he sold the priceless Christ for thirty pieces of silver. He was also a hypocrite. He is a classic example of a false disciple: he wasted his privileges, loved money more than he loved the Son of God, and was the hypocrite of hypocrites. Today many false disciples fill church pews. They feign love for Christ but at any given moment would sell Him for whatever was more valuable to them.

Lesson

III. THE DEFEAT OF THE DISCIPLES (vv. 50*b*-54, 56*a*)

A. The Action of the Multitudes (v. 50*b*)

"Then came they, and laid hands on Jesus, and took him."

After Judas identified Christ with a kiss, the authorities didn't waste any time seizing Him. John 18:12 says, "Then the band and the captain and officers of the Jews took Jesus, and bound him," as they would any prisoner. But before they could tie Him up, Luke 22:49 says, "When they [the disciples] who were about him saw what would follow, they said unto him, Lord, shall we smite with the sword?" There's nothing in Scripture to indicate that the Lord had the chance to answer before Peter acted.

B. The Arrogance of Peter (v. 51)

"Behold, one of those who were with Jesus stretched out his hand, and drew his sword [Gk., *machaira*], and struck a servant of the high priest's, and smote off his ear."

Neither Matthew, Mark, nor Luke tell us who drew his sword, but John does. Since John wrote his gospel long after this incident, it was safe for him to identify the assailant, who was Peter (John 18:10). When the other authors penned their gospels, Peter might have been exposed to reprisal from either the Jewish leaders or the Romans. John also identifies the high priest's servant: his name was Malchus. He served as an assistant to the high priest. Peter cut off his ear, but I am sure he was aiming for his head and missed. Obviously Malchus ducked. If Peter had his way, he would have fought his way through the mob.

What made Peter so bold? When the mob arrived in the garden and said they were seeking Jesus of Nazareth, the Lord said, "I am he," and they all fell to the ground (John 18:5-6). Perhaps Peter believed that if he got into trouble the Lord would knock them down again. In addition, he may have believed he had to fight to maintain his boast that he would never deny Christ even if he had to die. Peter's impetuous nature reacted violently to Christ's arrest.

Where did Peter get a sword? Luke 22:38 says, "[The disciples] said, Lord, behold, here are two swords. And he said unto them, It is enough." Some people believe the Lord meant that two swords were enough to win the battle, but I don't believe so.

C. The Approach of Christ (vv. 52-54, 56)

1. The declaration of non-violence (v. 52*a*)

"Then said Jesus unto him [Peter], Put up again thy sword into its place."

When the Lord told the disciples "it is enough" in reference to the two swords (Luke 22:38), He meant they were not to respond to their enemies by using those swords—as if to say, "Now, that's enough of that kind of talk." What prompted the disciples' response in Luke 22:38 was Christ's statement in verse 36: "He that hath a purse, let him take it, and likewise his bag; and he that hath no sword, let him sell his garment, and buy one." There the Lord was speaking in spiritual terms, but the disciples didn't understand that—they usually maintained a physical perspective on everything. Our Lord wanted them to understand that they would need extra spiritual resources when the time came to defend their lives.

a) The principle

> Second Corinthians 10:4 tells us, "The weapons of our warfare are not carnal [physical], but mighty through God to the pulling down of strongholds." So when the disciples said that they had two swords and the Lord said, "It is enough," He was implying that Christianity makes no advances with conventional weapons. There is no such thing as a holy war. Any so-called holy war in the name of Christ is utterly unholy. The kingdom of God does not advance by using fleshly weapons but by using spiritual weapons to tear down the dominion of Satan that reigns in the hearts of men and women. Peter was out of accord with spiritual reality when he started swinging his *machaira* around like a Roman soldier would wield his *rhomphaia* (a four-foot broadsword).

> In John 18:36 Jesus tells Pilate, "If my kingdom were of this world, then would my servants fight." What did He mean by that? That His kingdom is of another world. Christianity gains nothing by military might. Anything like the Crusades or terrorist activities in Ireland or the Middle East today are an affront to Christ.

b) The practice

> In John 18:11 Jesus tells Peter, "Put up thy sword into the sheath; the cup which my Father hath given me, shall I not drink it?" After Peter cut off Malchus's ear, Jesus "touched his ear, and healed him" (Luke 22:51). That is the only miracle recorded in Scripture where Jesus healed a fresh wound. Yet as far as we

know Malchus exhibited no faith in Christ. Jesus' miracles were sovereign: He performed them for people who showed faith in Him and for those who didn't.

At a time when a battle could have broken out between the mob and the disciples, Christ intervened. The Lord knew His work would be for naught had the eleven disciples been killed. In Luke 22:51 He says, "Permit ye thus far," which is better translated, "Stop! No more of this" (NASB). It is then that Christ gave Malchus a new ear.

2. The reasons for non-violence (vv. 52*b*-54, 56*a*)

The Lord gives us some important reasons for avoiding violence.

a) Violence is fatal (v. 52*b*)

"All they that take the sword shall perish with the sword."

People who use a sword for personal acts of violence will be executed. In that verse our Lord is advocating capital punishment.

(1) Genesis 9:6—"Whoso sheddeth man's blood, by man shall his blood be shed." If you kill someone, you will die. That's God's law, and Jesus reiterates it in Matthew 26:52. When someone takes a life, the government has the right to take his life. God established that divine law to preserve society and the sanctity of human life.

(2) Romans 13:4—"[The government] beareth not the sword in vain." God has given the government the right to take the life of murderers.

When the apostle Paul was held captive by the Romans, he appealed to the law, saying, "If I be an offender, or have committed anything worthy of death, I refuse not to die" (Acts 25:11). He upheld the law of God.

It is unacceptable for anyone, except the authorized executioner, to take a life. It doesn't matter if something is unjust, inequitable, or ungodly; no one has the right to personal vengeance because of it. That's what Christ was telling Peter. If he were to kill one person in the mob, he would forfeit his own life. Under no circumstances does a Christian have the right to decide on his own to take a life, even if his intent is to defend Christ's honor. That doesn't mean you don't have the right to defend yourself or your loved ones from someone who's trying to kill you. But any act of vengeance against someone should bring about the penalty for murder.

b) Violence is foolish (v. 53)

"Thinkest thou that I cannot now pray to my Father, and he shall presently give me more than twelve legions of angels?"

Do you see how foolish vengeance is? Peter didn't have to fight; if Christ wanted help He could have asked God to send Him more than twelve legions of angels, or more than 72,000 angels. According to 2 Kings 19:35, one angel killed 185,000 Assyrians by himself. Imagine how much damage 72,000 angels could do! Peter didn't need to defend the kingdom of God, because the Lord is not without His own resources.

"Thinkest thou that I cannot now [Gk. *arti*, "immediately"]" means Jesus could have asked the Father for help, and He would have responded immediately. But Christ did not ask for help because He didn't need it. Christianity does not conquer that way. God will conquer in His own time, by His own way, and in His own power.

Jesus yielded voluntarily to the murderous plot. The arrest itself was not outside the law since the Jewish leaders worked within some semblance of a legal framework. They weren't going to lynch Him in the garden—they were going to give Him a trial. The government brought Jesus to trial, but the entire affair was unfair and illegal. Nonetheless, it was an act of government, and Peter had no right to take personal vengeance against it. If God wanted to defend Christ He would have. When governments do things that are unfair, or when people do things in the name of the government that are unfair, we have no right to retaliate. If the Lord wants to deliver us, He will. But if we retaliate with violence, we will bring the death penalty on ourselves.

c) Violence undermines the plan of God (vv. 54, 56a)

"How, then, shall the scriptures be fulfilled, that thus it must be? . . . But all this was done, that the scriptures of the prophets might be fulfilled."

According to Scripture, Jesus had to be taken captive and led away like a sheep to slaughter. Sheep do not battle the shepherd; they are led to slaughter quietly and peacefully. Christ had to be betrayed, as Psalm 41:9 says: "Mine own familiar friend, in whom I trusted, who did eat of my bread, hath lifted up his heel against me." Zechariah 11:12 says, "They weighed for my price thirty pieces of silver." It had to happen as Psalm 22 and Isaiah 53 said it would.

Peter boasted too loudly, prayed too little, slept too much, and acted too quickly. And he was still in error when he tried to fight against the mob.

D. The Abandonment of the Disciples (v. 56b)

"All the disciples forsook him, and fled."

The Greek word translated "all" is emphatic. Matthew 26:56 becomes a fulfillment of verse 31: "All ye shall be offended because of me this night." The disciples fled out of fear. The Lord didn't fight back, and He wouldn't let Peter fight. Once the Lord was arrested, they became afraid. And although the Lord forced the Roman soldiers and Jewish leaders to admit that they were interested in arresting Jesus of Nazareth only, the disciples were sure they would come after them eventually. They didn't trust Jesus to deliver them, so they ran.

A Mysterious Young Man

I'm not sure how Christ would have rescued the disciples had they not run, but I do know that one man was delivered. Mark 14:50-51 says, "They all forsook him, and fled. And there followed [Jesus] a certain young man." We don't know the identity of this young man. Obviously he was someone who cared about Christ. Verse 51 says he had "a linen cloth cast about his naked body." That doesn't mean he was stark naked; he undoubtedly was wearing a loin cloth over which he had thrown a linen cloth. That means he probably had come hurriedly. Perhaps he had seen the crowd moving through the streets and suspected something. Some believe he may have lived in the house where Christ and the disciples celebrated the Passover. There are those who conjecture that the house belonged to John Mark, and that the young man was John Mark. We don't know for sure, but we do know that after the disciples fled, this unidentified person followed Christ. The narrative continues, "The young men [in the crowd] laid hold on him; and he left the linen cloth, and fled from them naked" (Mark 14:51-52). Some in the crowd assumed he was a follower of Christ, so they seized him. But he got away by running out from under his linen cloth.

Why the Holy Spirit included that incident in Mark's gospel is difficult to understand. One thing we can know is that since the Lord allowed this man to escape, He would have planned some way to deliver the disciples out of the clutches of the crowd if they had remained faithful and followed Him. But the disciples never experienced that deliverance because they fled.

The disciples couldn't handle the pressure of their trial. They claimed they would follow Jesus to death if need be. They claimed they would never be offended by Him or deny Him. But that didn't happen. When the trial arrived and their lives were on the line, they ran. As we look at that incident we wonder how they could have done that to the Son of God. But once we look at our own unfaithfulness we realize we too have run from trials and abandoned Christ. Have you been unfaithful, refusing to stand with Him when there was a price to pay?

Characteristics of Defective Disciples

1. They are unprepared

The disciples slept instead of praying. Why? Because they believed they were safe. They confused their good intentions with strength and courage. Being overconfident, they didn't believe they needed to pray. They didn't take to heart the marvelous promises Jesus gave them in John 13-16. They didn't listen to His prayer in John 17 as He asked the Father to keep them and uphold them. By ignoring the Word and prayer, they were unprepared. If you ignore those two things, I'll guarantee that you'll be unprepared, too. People will defect when they're weak in the Word and prayer.

2. They are impulsive

The disciples acted on impulse rather than reason—on emotion rather than revelation. They didn't think through what was right or reason what was best. So they reacted to the moment. Out came Peter's sword, and off went Malchus's ear. The next thing you know, they ran. They were completely impulsive with no sense of how to respond properly.

My fear is that many Christians are unprepared. They do not have a biblical mind-set and are not in consistent communion with God. Every believer should develop an open line of communication with God. They need to be in tune to what God would have them do in any given situation. People who aren't communicating with God react to situations impulsively and emotionally. They are constantly dependent on how they feel. Every believer must so develop his Christian walk that his involuntary and immediate responses are godly. But that can happen only when you're controlled by the Word of God and the Spirit of God. If you're a victim of your own anxieties, you're going to have problems.

3. They are impatient

Defective disciples can't wait for God's deliverance. The young man in Mark 14:51 was almost captured, but God freed him by His providence. Had the disciples waited on God, they might have seen a great miracle delivering them from harm. Many Christians act like that today. Rather than wait for God to deliver us, we take the easy route of escape and bring reproach upon the Savior because we weren't up to the task. If we endured each trial to its conclusion, we would see God's deliverance and offer Him praise as a result.

4. They are carnal

Disciples who are likely to defect rely on their fleshly power and weapons. But when they lose those fleshly resources they don't know what to do or whom to trust.

In summation, defective disciples are inconsistent. They promise all kinds of things, but they just don't produce the promised results.

IV. THE TRIUMPH OF THE SAVIOR (v. 55)

Matthew's special joy is to preserve Christ's glory no matter how ugly the scene appears. Look at what Christ endured: the world hated Him and wanted Him dead. One of His disciples, who spent three years with Him, sold Him for the price of a slave. His other disciples fled when their lives were threatened. At first glance that doesn't say much for Christ. A sequence of events like that appears to tear down Christ's glory and rob Him of any majesty. But on the other hand, by looking carefully at the words of the Spirit of God, we see that the opposite is true. In spite of all that happened, Christ was triumphant.

A. In His Confrontation with the Crowd

1. He established His power (John 18:4-8)

Sometime near the moment when Judas arrived and kissed Christ a remarkable event occurred. John 18:4 says that Jesus "went forth, and said unto them, Whom seek ye?" A kiss was unnecessary—Jesus wasn't hiding. Jesus stripped Judas of any satisfaction over having accomplished anything meaningful. The narrative continues, "They answered him, Jesus, of Nazareth. Jesus saith unto them, I am he. And Judas also, who betrayed him, stood with them. As soon, then, as he had said unto them, I am he, they went backward, and fell to the ground" (vv. 5-6). Hundreds of people hit the ground flat on their backs. With one response Christ showed who was in control. Initially you might consider Jesus as a victim, but He wasn't. They were able to stand up again only because He allowed them to. Verses 7-8 continue: "Then asked he them again, Whom seek ye? And they said, Jesus, of Nazareth. Jesus answered, I have told you that I am he; if, therefore, ye seek me, let these go their way." Even then Jesus was working out the disciples' deliverance. He had total control over that mob. But the mob was so mindless that they stood back up and continued with the arrest as if nothing had happened. Judas was possessed by Satan, and the hour belonged to him and the powers of darkness (Luke 22:53). Satan's plan was allowed to work for a time, but Jesus was always in control.

2. He exposed their evil (Matthew 26:55)

Matthew said, "In that same hour said Jesus to the multitudes, Are ye come out as against a thief [lit., "robber"] with swords and clubs to take me? I sat daily with you teaching in the temple, and ye laid no hold on me." There are some powerful implications in what Christ says in verse 55. He questioned their wasted opportunities to arrest Him on Monday, Tuesday, Wednesday, and possibly Thursday when He was with them in the Temple. Why didn't they seize Him then? Jesus, by asking them that question, is revealing that they are the robbers. They could have taken Him any day during the week had they justification to do so. But they knew they had no right to. They feared the people, who believed Him to be the Messiah. Jesus unmasked their evil motives. He wasn't the robber; they were. They were being led by Satan, which Christ affirmed when He said, "This is your hour, and the power of darkness" (Luke 22:53). God, by His sovereign design, gave hell its moment—from early Friday morning until just after dawn on Sunday when Christ left the tomb.

The leaders didn't take Christ earlier because it wasn't the right time. But when the time was right the mob served as hell's agents. Christ had a twofold intent in verse 55: to show the mob that what they did was evil (which they knew or they would have arrested Him in public) and to affirm that they were acting under Satan's direction.

We see Christ triumphant as He faces the crowd. God controlled everything. The crowd was a victim, falling down when they were confronted by the Son of God.

B. In His Confrontation with Judas

Jesus told Judas to get on with what he came to do (v. 50). Christ offered no struggle, anger, or wrath. With absolute calmness, commitment, and trust He put Himself in God's hands. He didn't react as a criminal would. He didn't react as an innocent man would and proclaim His innocence.

C. In His Confrontation with Peter

Peter had no trust—he didn't understand His spiritual resources. Christ did, which is why He was totally calm. Jesus placed Himself in the Father's hand. His heavenly loyalty was unfamiliar to Peter and the disciples. They were disloyal, and they ran as a result; He was loyal and stayed despite a temptation that was infinitely stronger than theirs.

Conclusion

Where are you in the scene? Do you identify with the rejecting mob? Jesus said, "He that is not with me is against me" (Matt. 12:30). Do you belong with the unjust, mindless, cowardly, profane group of people who deny Christ? Perhaps you're a false disciple who pretends to love God and Christ, but the truth is you're after what you can get. If you can't get it, you'd sell Jesus if something better came along. Or do you identify with the disciples, who were so weak that once the temptation became fierce, they ran and lost the battle? Or, do you stand victorious with the triumphant Savior, willing to endure whatever comes along?

Focusing on the Facts

1. How did the disciples initially respond to Jesus' arrest (Matt. 26:51; Luke 22:49; see pp. 79-80)?
2. Why did Peter cut off Malchus's ear (see p. 80)?
3. What caused Peter's initial boldness (see p. 80)?
4. Explain Christ's response in Luke 22:38 when the disciples told Him they had two swords (see pp. 80-81).
5. How did Christ remedy Peter's action (Luke 22:51; see pp. 81-82)?
6. What was our Lord advocating in Matthew 26:52? Why (see p. 82)?
7. Is there ever justification for taking the life of another? Explain (see p. 83).
8. According to Matthew 26:53, why didn't Christ need Peter's help (see p. 83)?
9. How should all believers respond to the government when it does things that are unfair (see p. 84)?
10. How did the Old Testament indicate that Christ's capture would take place (see p. 84)?
11. When did the disciples become afraid? What did they do (Matt. 26:56; see p. 84)?
12. What is the significance of the events surrounding the young man referred to in Mark 14:50-52 (see p. 85)?
13. What are the characteristics of a defective disciple? Explain the significance of each one (see pp. 86-87).
14. How did Christ demonstrate that He was in control of the events surrounding His arrest (John 18:4-8; see pp. 87-88)?
15. How did Christ expose the mob's evil motives (Matt. 26:55; see pp. 88-89)?

Pondering the Principles

1. Read Romans 13:2. In light of Christ's command to Peter in Matthew 26:52, how should you respond to the government when you disagree with its decisions? Perhaps you have experienced unfair treatment from the government. How did you respond? Read Acts 16:20-25. What lesson can you learn from the response of Paul and Silas to the injustice they experienced? How will you respond the next time you're treated unfairly?

2. Review the section on the characteristics of a defective disciple (see pp. 86-87). Are you unprepared for the temptations you might face in the future? Are you impulsive—reacting emotionally to a situation before determining how God would want you to react? Are you impatient, wondering when God will answer your prayer or deliver you out of trouble? Are you carnal, depending on your own resources rather than trusting in God? If you answered yes to any of those questions, you are in danger of abandoning the Lord. Look up the following verses: Psalm 27:11-14, Matthew 26:41, 2 Corinthians 10:3-4, Colossians 1:9-12. Match each of those passages with the characteristic it addresses. Determine what you must do to change.

6
The Illegal, Unjust Trials of Jesus—Part 1

Outline

Introduction
A. The System of Justice
    1. The Sanhedrin
    2. The great Sanhedrin
       a) Its attributes
          (1) Wise justices
          (2) Procedural guarantees
             (*a*) The right to a public trial
             (*b*) The right to self-defense
             (*c*) The right to hear witnesses
          (3) Prescribed executions
       b) Its abuses
B. The Trials of Christ
    1. Two trials
    2. Three phases

Lesson
I. The Illegal, Unjust Confrontation (John 18:12-13, 19-24)
    A. The Significance of the Hearing Before Annas (John 18:12-13)
       1. Typological
       2. Political
    B. The Sequence of the Hearing Before Annas (John 18:19-24)
       1. Annas's circumvention of proper legal procedure (v. 19)
       2. Christ's call for proper legal procedure (vv. 20-21)
       3. An officer's conflict with proper legal procedure (v. 22)
       4. Jesus' affirmation of proper legal procedure (v. 23)
       5. Annas's concealment of proper legal procedure (v. 24)

Introduction

Matthew 26:57-66 is the record of the illegal, unjust trials of Jesus. I want to lay a foundation so we might understand how unfair they really were. In spite of their nature, those trials demonstrate Christ's perfect majesty.

A. The System of Justice

The Jewish people have prided themselves on their sense of fairness, equity, and justice—and rightly so. They have laid a foundation of justice that has benefited the world. The system of justice practiced in America traces some of its origins to the Judaic justice system, as do many other equitable systems around the world.

The Jewish system of jurisprudence was predicated primarily on one Old Testament passage. Deuteronomy 16:18-20 says, "Judges and officers shalt thou make thee in all thy gates, which the Lord thy God giveth thee, throughout thy tribes, and they shall judge the people with just judgment. Thou shalt not distort justice. Thou shalt not respect persons, neither take a bribe; for a bribe doth blind the eyes of the wise and pervert the words of the righteous. That which is altogether just shalt thou follow, that thou mayest live and inherit the land which the Lord thy God giveth thee." That is God's standard for judgment and justice: local judges judging the people with fairness and righteousness, never distorting what is true, never being partial, and never taking bribes. Throughout the history of the Jewish people, that standard was the basis of their system of jurisprudence.

1. The Sanhedrin

   To practically apply Deuteronomy 16:18-20, the nation formed local councils in any region where 120 men served as heads of families. That large a community could support a synagogue as well. The local councils became known as Sanhedrin, which is a Hebrew transliteration of a Greek word meaning "sitting together." Each Sanhedrin was made up of twenty-three men who sat together to make judgments and decide civil and criminal issues. An odd number was necessary so that there could always be a majority in any close decision. The twenty-three men were chosen from the elders of the village, and they acted as judges and jury in all matters. (Figures come from Simon Greenleaf's *Testimony of the Evangelists* [Jersey City, N.J.: Frederick P. Linn, 1881], p. 579).

2. The great Sanhedrin

   a) Its attributes

      The great Sanhedrin ruled in Jerusalem, the capital city and religious center of Israel. It was composed of seventy men plus the high priest. Twenty-four were chief priests, twenty-four were elders, and twenty-three were scribes. This council was the final court for appeal. Anyone who believed that a verdict rendered at a lower level was unfair could appeal to the Sanhedrin in Jerusalem. Under the right conditions they could gain a hearing. The great Sanhedrin was the highest ruling body in Israel.

      (1) Wise justices

         Some of the men who served on the court were chosen from the local councils on the basis of their wisdom. Others served their apprenticeships as pupils of Sanhedrin members. After first learning about court procedure they were then invited to serve as judges themselves.

(2) Procedural guarantees

A person under prosecution had three guarantees.

(*a*) The right to a public trial

There could be no secret trials. Every trial was to be held in public so that no one could be framed and then be penalized or executed. In that way the judges were constantly under the scrutiny of the populace, who were able to attend and know what was going on. All fair courts today have maintained the same procedure.

(*b*) The right to self-defense

There was to be a defender—someone who provided a defense for the accused.

(*c*) The right to hear witnesses

No one could be convicted of anything unless proved guilty by two or three witnesses. A solid case could be built only on the evidence of more than one witness.

Those basic rights remain with us today and are guaranteed by our court system. Those rights are important to know as we examine the trials of Christ. As you will see, the Sanhedrin violated all three plus many others.

The Fate of a False Witness

Bearing false witness was a serious crime, and punishment for it was swift. Anyone who gave false testimony was punished with the very penalty the accused would have received. Suppose you came into the court as witness to a murder. When your false testimony was found out, you would receive the death penalty yourself. Deuteronomy 19:16-19 says, "If a false witness rise up against any man to testify against him that which is wrong, then both the men, between whom the controversy is, shall stand before the Lord, before the priests and the judges, who shall be in those days; and the judges shall make diligent inquiry; and, behold, if the witness be a false witness, and hath testified falsely against his brother, then shall ye do unto him, as he had thought to have done unto his brother. So shalt thou put the evil away from among you." People were discouraged from giving false testimony by the penalty they would incur if they were caught.

(3) Prescribed executions

In any case deserving a death sentence, the execution could not be carried out until the third day. (The first day was considered to be the day the sentence was rendered.) The council would reconvene on the third day to reaffirm the death sentence and execute the accused that same day. The second day was necessary to be sure that all the evidence had been examined and that there was no further need of testimony.

The witnesses whose testimony brought about the death penalty had to cast the first stones in the execution (Deut. 17:7). That was another reason the witness wanted to be certain his testimony was true. If not, he would be guilty not only of perjury but also of murder. The Lord had that in mind when the scribes and Pharisees wanted Him to make a judgment regarding a woman caught in adultery (John 8:3-5). He told them, "He that is without sin among you, let him first cast a stone at her" (v. 7). That would have been the procedure at a criminal trial had she been found guilty. Those witnesses would have been responsible to cast the first stones. But Jesus gave them a condition: they could do it only if they had never sinned.

Peeking Inside the Courtroom

Simon Greenleaf was a famous professor of law at Harvard University in the last century. His book *The Testimony of the Evangelists* (Jersey City, N.J.: Frederick P. Linn, 1881) contains a section written by an eminent lawyer of the French bar on the Sanhedrin trial procedure. This excerpt will give us some indication of what should have transpired in the trial of Christ.

1. The witnesses

The lawyer writes, "On the day of the trial, the executive officers of justice cause the accused person to make his appearance. At the feet of the Elders were placed men who, under the name of auditors, or candidates, followed regularly the sittings of the Council" (p. 581). The council was audited by objective men, who scrutinized all procedures to verify that they conformed to justice and equity. The lawyer continues, "The papers in the case were read; and the witnesses were called in succession. The president addressed this exhortation to each of them: 'It is not conjectures, or whatever public rumour has brought to thee, that we ask of thee; consider that a great responsibility rests upon thee: that we are not occupied by an affair, like a case of pecuniary interest, in which the injury may be repaired. If thou causest the condemnation of a person unjustly accused, his blood, and the blood of all the posterity of him, of whom thou wilt have deprived the earth, will fall upon thee; God will demand of thee an account, as He demanded of Cain an account of the blood of Abel. Speak' " (pp. 581-82). That concept filtered down to present-day courts through the years. In U.S. courts the witness is required to place his hand on a Bible and to swear before God to "tell the truth, the whole truth, and nothing but the truth." The Jewish courts laid the bloodguiltiness on the witness who brought false testimony against a man in a case deserving the death sentence.

Furthermore, the lawyer writes, "A woman could not be a witness, because she would not have the courage to give the first blow to the condemned person; nor could a child, that is irresponsible, nor a slave, nor a man of bad character, nor one whose infirmities prevent the full enjoyment of his physical and moral faculties. The simple confession of an individual against himself, or the declaration, however renowned, would not decide a condemnation" (p. 582). That's important to note: Jewish law stated that no person could testify against himself, and on the basis of that single testimony be held guilty. Similarly, U.S. court systems protect against self-incrimination. The lawyer adds that the Sanhedrin stated, "We hold it as fundamental, that no one shall prejudice himself. If a man accuses himself before a tribunal, we must not believe him, unless the fact is attested by two other witnesses" (p. 582).

The lawyer also writes, "The witnesses were to attest to the identity of the party, and to depose to the month, day, hour, and circumstances of the crime. After an examination of the proofs, these judges who believed the party innocent stated their reasons; those who believed him guilty spoke afterwards, and with the greatest moderation. If one of the auditors, or candidates, was entrusted by the accused with his defense, or if he wished in his own name to present any elucidations in favour of innocence, he was admitted to the seat, from which he addressed the judges and the people. But this liberty was not granted to him, if his opinion was in favour of condemning" (p. 582). Someone other than a judge could speak only if it was in behalf of the accused's innocence, and not in behalf of his guilt. They wanted to avoid an emotional response that could bring about a guilty verdict.

2. The judgment

The lawyer writes, "When the accused person himself wished to speak, they gave the most profound attention. When the discussion was finished, one of the judges recapitulated the case; they removed all the spectators; two scribes took down the votes of the judges; one of them noted those which were in favour of the accused; and the other, those which condemned him. Eleven votes, out of twenty-three, were sufficient to acquit; but it required thirteen to convict" (pp. 582-83).

3. The punishment

The lawyer continues, "If a majority of votes acquitted, the accused was discharged instantly; if he was to be punished, the judges postponed pronouncing sentence till the third day; during the intermediate day, they could not be occupied with anything but the case, and they abstained from eating freely" (p. 583). The judges fasted, which indicates they would never hold a trial of this nature the day before a feast day, otherwise they would be fasting during a feast, thus violating Jewish law. That was another violation in the trial of Christ. The judges were to refrain "from wine, liquors, and everything which might render their minds less capable of reflection" (p. 583).

The lawyer details the following procedure: "On the morning of the third day they returned to the judgment seat. Each judge, who had not changed his opinion, said, I continue of the same opinion and condemn; any one, who at first condemned, might at this sitting acquit; but he who at once acquitted was not allowed to condemn. If a majority condemned, two magistrates immediately accompanied the condemned person to the place of punishment" (p. 583). They executed him on the same day they sentenced him. That was consistent with Ecclesiastes 8:11, which states that when there is swift punishment, there will be decreasing crime.

The lawyer continues, "The Elders did not descend from their seats; they placed at the entrance of the judgment hall an officer of justice with a small flag in his hand; a second officer, on horseback, followed the prisoner, and constantly kept looking back to the place of departure. During this interval, if any person came to announce to the elders any new evidence favorable to the prisoner, the first officer waved his flag, and the second one, as soon as he perceived it, brought back the prisoner. If the prisoner declared to the magistrates, that he recollected some reasons which had escaped him, they brought him before the judges no less than five times. If no incident occurred, the procession advanced slowly, preceded by a herald who, in a loud voice, addressed the people thus: 'This man (stating his name and surname) is led to punishment for such a crime; the witnesses who have sworn against him are such and such persons; if any one has evidence to give in his favour, let him come forth quickly.'. . . At some distance from the place of punishment, they urged the prisoner to confess his crime, and they made him drink a stupefying beverage, in order to render the approach of death less terrible" (pp. 583-84).

b) Its abuses

Once you analyze the procedure of a Sanhedrin trial, you could easily conclude that any individual accused of a crime was safe in the Sanhedrin's hands. They had a tremendous sense of justice mixed with mercy. Built into their system were safeguards to protect the innocent party. The accused had abundant opportunity to bring in new testimony. That bearing false witness was such a serious crime acted as a good preventative. Add to that the judges' day-long fast and the period of reflection, and a trial before the Sanhedrin appears to be a winning proposition for any wrongly accused individual.

But the Sanhedrin never was a safe environment for Christ. In His trial the Sanhedrin violated every single law governing proper procedure in a criminal trial. As such, the trial of Jesus Christ is the most unjust trial in human history. The great Sanhedrin condemned to death the only completely innocent person who ever lived. It was a mockery of justice. The axiom of the Sanhedrin was to save, not to destroy life. But that ideal was jettisoned in the case of Christ. No criminal trial was to be conducted at night, but Christ's trial was. Before condemning a criminal the judges were to fast a day before the execution, but those who condemned Christ didn't—they killed Him the same day. Witnesses were required to testify against the accused, but none were found who had truthful testimony against Christ. The accused had the right of defense, but that wasn't allowed in the case of Christ.

B. The Trials of Christ

1. Two trials

Jesus basically received two trials: a religious, Jewish trial and a secular, Roman trial. The Jews were an occupied people. Only Roman courts had the right to execute anyone—the Jewish courts couldn't. The Jewish leaders could condemn Jesus to death, but they couldn't execute Him. Whatever verdict they rendered in their religious trial had to be one recognized by the Romans. That is why there were two trials. The Jews had to present the evidence from their trial to the Romans. Before they would execute Christ, the Romans needed to examine the evidence against Jesus to determine if He indeed had committed a crime.

101

2. Three phases

The Jewish trial and the Roman trial each had three phases. So Jesus was actually involved in six different trials. The Jewish trial began when Jesus was taken to Annas. Annas sent Him to Caiaphas and the Sanhedrin in the middle of the night. The third phase took place before Caiaphas and the Sanhedrin just after dawn in an attempt to legitimize their evil. After the religious leaders were done with Christ, they sent Him to the Roman governor, Pontius Pilate. After Pilate questioned Him, he sent Him to Herod Antipas, who ruled over Galilee. Herod sent Him back to Pilate, who in turn condemned Him to death. Those were the three phases of the Roman trial. Both the Jews and Romans violated rules of justice, truth, equity, and fairness, committing horrendous crimes against an innocent man.

That series of trials led to the execution of Jesus Christ. The Jews wanted Him dead, so they had to invent a means to bring about His death. They predetermined the sentence; they just needed a crime to fit it.

Lesson

I. THE ILLEGAL, UNJUST CONFRONTATION (John 18:12-13, 19-24)

Matthew 26:57 says, "They that laid hold on Jesus led him away to Caiaphas, the high priest, where the scribes and the elders were assembled." Although it's true that Christ was led to Caiaphas, Matthew doesn't discuss the phase of the trial that occurred first. John 18 details what happened in that first phase—the initial arraignment.

A. The Significance of the Hearing Before Annas (John 18:12-13)

"Then the band [Gk., *speira*—the Roman cohort, as many as six hundred men] and the captain [Gk., *chiliarchos*] and officers of the Jews took Jesus, and bound him, and led him away to Annas first."

The gospels offer us a composite of the life of Christ. In a sense they are like four different paintings, each of which emphasizes different features of His life.

1. Typological

Psalm 118:27 says, "Bind the sacrifice with cords, even unto the horns of the altar." Every sacrifice was in a sense a type of Christ. He was bound even as Isaac was bound to be sacrificed (Genesis 22:9). Christ was bound as a criminal. He was about to be offered as a sacrifice for all mankind.

2. Political

The reason Christ was taken to Annas first is that apparently Annas was the brains behind the leaders' scheme to kill Christ. He despised Jesus because He was a threat to his security, power, and prestige. He resented Jesus' holiness because he was utterly unholy. He resented Jesus' perfection because he was utterly vile. Everything about Jesus caused him anger. Of course Satan was directing Annas's plan. Annas was just one in a cast of characters being manipulated by hell.

The soldiers took Jesus to Annas's house. That was illegal because it happened at night and in a house instead of the Judgment Hall. Annas had been high priest for about a five-year span, but that had been twenty years before. His son-in-law, Caiaphas, was the official high priest that year (John 18:13).

B. The Sequence of the Hearing Before Annas (John 18:19-24)

1. Annas's circumvention of proper legal procedure (v. 19)

"The high priest then asked Jesus of his disciples, and of his doctrine."

Annas wanted to know what Jesus taught, how widespread His movement was, and who followed Him. Annas violated all sense of justice with his questions. When a person was arraigned in a court of law, he was to be told

103

the crime of which he was accused. But Annas asked general questions about Jesus' movement in an attempt to uncover a crime. He already had a sentence; he just needed a crime to match it. This was an illegal and unjust hearing, and Jesus' answer affirms that.

2. Christ's call for proper legal procedure (vv. 20-21)

"Jesus answered him, I spoke openly to the world; I ever taught in the synagogue, and in the temple, where the Jews always resort; and in secret have I said nothing. Why asketh thou me? Ask them who heard me, what I have said unto them; behold, they know what I said."

If Annas had a case, he should have presented witnesses and not asked Christ. According to the law, Jesus couldn't incriminate Himself. Here He called for proper legal procedure. He exposed the evil injustice of Annas. Everything Jesus taught was said openly and publicly. Plenty of people had heard Him; Annas only needed to call them as witnesses.

Annas was embarrassed and frustrated. His intentions had been unmasked. He was no match for the infinite mind of Jesus. When the tension in the air gets this thick, someone will eventually break it, as happened here.

3. An officer's conflict with proper legal procedure (v. 22)

"When he had thus spoken, one of the officers who stood by struck Jesus with the palm of his hand, saying, Answereth thou the high priest so?"

Jesus had unmasked Annas as a violator of the laws of justice. This officer—in his desire to defend his master, who had just lost face—slapped Jesus.

4. Jesus' affirmation of proper legal procedure (v. 23)

"Jesus answered him, If I have spoken evil, bear witness of the evil; but if well, why smitest thou me?"

The Lord offered no emotional retaliation, in contrast to when Paul was brought before the Sanhedrin in Acts 23. Paul testified that he lived with a clear conscience before God (v. 1). That so upset the high priest that he had one of his servants slap Paul on the mouth. Paul retorted, "God shall smite thee, thou whited wall" (v. 3). That sounds like something I might say! But Jesus didn't react that way. First Peter 2:23 says, "When he was reviled, [He] reviled not again." The hour of His death was at hand, and He was resolute about going to the cross. He already had settled that issue back in the garden. There was nothing to be gained with an angry retort. That's why He said, "If I have spoken evil, bear witness of the evil; but if well, why smitest thou me?" There is no answer to that question. Jesus always knew the right thing to say.

5. Annas's concealment of proper legal procedure (v. 24)

"Annas had sent him bound unto Caiaphas, the high priest."

Annas was finished. What could he do? It was the middle of the night. We know it was before 3:00 A.M., because the period of cockcrow ended at that time, and Peter hadn't yet denied Christ. Annas attempted a clandestine arraignment and couldn't accomplish a thing, except to become embarrassed. So Jesus was sent to Caiaphas without an indictment.

The confrontation with Annas was illegal and unjust. What was illegal about it? It took place in the middle of the night. There were no witnesses. There were no charges. Annas had no legal authority—he wasn't even an official prosecutor. And his home was an improper place to hold an arraignment.

II. THE ILLEGAL, UNJUST CONVENING (Matthew 26:57)

"They that had laid hold on Jesus led him away to Caiaphas, the high priest, where the scribes and the elders were assembled."

Caiaphas was equally as wretched as Annas. He was possessive, power-hungry, and greedy. He hated truth, righteousness, and holiness. That's why he hated Jesus Christ. In the dark of night Jesus was transported from the house of Annas to the house of Caiaphas, which was located near the Temple.

A. The People

The scribes and elders had been gathering together at Caiaphas's place while Jesus was at the house of Annas. Mark 14:53 says that all the scribes and elders were there. However, based on a passage in Luke, I suggest that at least one of them wasn't present. Now that doesn't violate the use of "all" in Mark. They were all gathered in the sense that a great number of them were present. I believe Joseph of Arimathea was not there. Luke 23:50-51 says Joseph "was a member of the council, a good and righteous man (he had not consented to their plan and action)" (NASB). He was not there to vote. But, apart from Joseph, the vast majority of council members were prepared to convict Christ. I'm sure some of them didn't even realize what was going on. They were the pawns of Satan.

B. The Place

Luke 22:54 says they met in the house of Caiaphas. Verse 55 tells us that there was a courtyard as part of the grounds. Men like Caiaphas lived in large houses because they were wealthy. So Christ was taken across the courtyard into a large room adjacent to it.

In the courtyard some soldiers had gathered around a fire (v. 55). Matthew 26:58 says, "Peter followed him [Christ] afar off unto the high priest's court, and went in, and sat with the guards, to see the end." Peter was caught between cowardice and curiosity. He wasn't brave enough to step out for Christ, but he was concerned enough to stand in the background. It is in that environment that he denied Jesus Christ. While in the courtyard he no doubt could look through the doors or windows of the large room to see what happened as Christ was confronted by Caiaphas and the Sanhedrin.

The law of Israel stated that no one was to be tried in any place other than the Hall of Judgment, which was located in the Temple complex. Also, trials were to be held during the day. And they were to be public. The Sanhedrin did hold a brief trial at dawn in the Hall of Judgment to present some form of legal procedure to such illegal proceedings.

C. The Purpose

The Sanhedrin had to originate charges against Jesus. But that was a violation of law because the Sanhedrin could act only as judge and jury, not as prosecutor. They were supposed to investigate charges previously brought against the accused. Since Christ's session with Annas failed to exact a charge, they had no case to judge. So they had to act as prosecutors first and invent a crime before they could try it. The one thing they did have was a sentence—they just needed a crime to go with it.

Everything about the trial of Christ was illegal. It was not supposed to take place at night, or in the house of the high priest. There was no crime. The Sanhedrin was not supposed to act as prosecutor. No one was to be tried on a feast day. And bribery was not to be tolerated, yet that is how Jesus was betrayed by Judas. All the illegalities of the trial before Annas were compounded in the convening of the Sanhedrin in the house of Caiaphas.

III. THE ILLEGAL, UNJUST CONSPIRACY (Matthew 26:59-61)

A. The Search for False Witnesses (vv. 59-60a)

"The chief priests, and elders, and all the council, sought false witness against Jesus, to put him to death, but found none; yea, though many false witnesses came, yet found they none."

The council didn't want to find out the truth; they wanted to put Him to death. The only way an innocent man could be killed was to find people to lie about him. They had to be liars to convict Jesus, who was a perfect man—God in human flesh. Perfection violates nothing. There never was a crime.

So the council sought liars to do the very thing their law condemned with such ferocity. Their passions were controlled by hatred and dominated by Satan and his demonic forces. The predetermined plan of God was that Jesus die for the sins of the world, and these men were unknowingly swept up in that plan. They were actually seeking the testimony of false witnesses—the very thing they had spent their lives trying to protect people from! It is unthinkable that judges would do that, but they did. Jesus never received a fair trial. He was not condemned because of something He had done; He was condemned out of hate.

Not surprisingly, no one could give a plausible testimony. There were many people who wanted to, and I'm sure hell generated all it could, but nothing made sense. Worse than that, they couldn't find any two to agree. It is difficult for liars to agree since they have no facts to deal with. Mark 14:56 says, "Many bore false witness against him, but their witness agreed not together."

B.   The Selection of False Witnesses (vv. 60*b*-61)

"At the last came two false witnesses, and said, This fellow said, I am able to destroy the temple of God, and to build it in three days."

All they could come up with was "this fellow said." That's nothing but a generalization. Mark 14:57-58 says, "There arose certain, and bore false witness against him, saying, we heard him say, I will destroy this temple that is made with hands, and within three days I will build another made without hands." Look at the difference between those two testimonies. The one in Matthew claimed Jesus said, "I am able to destroy the temple of God, and to build it in three days." The one in Mark's record claimed He said, "I will destroy this temple that is made with hands, and within three days I will build another made without hands." Even they don't agree. What did Jesus actually say? John 2:19 tells us: "Destroy this temple, and in three days I will raise it up." Verse 21 tells us He was referring to "the temple of his body." The false witnesses twisted what Jesus actually said.

The testimony of those two witnesses should never have been admitted. As mentioned earlier, a witness had to know the year, month, day, hour, and location of the supposed crime. Also, there were strict rules regarding the limitations of disagreement that could be tolerated between witnesses.

Conclusion

If I didn't know Jesus Christ was perfect and absolutely sinless and that He was the Son of God as He claimed, this incident alone would convince me He was. Satan entered Judas. It was the hour of darkness. Satan and his most powerful and resourceful demons were after an accusation against Jesus. When all earth and all hell, energized by supernatural resources and intelligence, can't find anything against Jesus Christ, there isn't anything to find. The trials of Christ are as great an apologetic for the perfection of Jesus Christ as is found anywhere in the pages of Scripture. If Jesus had ever done anything wrong, they would have found it. But there was no crime. Jesus was God in human flesh—and no less.

The trials were illegal. Witnesses were bribed, and they misrepresented what Jesus said and meant. Jewish law never allowed for the execution of an accused man based on what he said. Jesus was allowed no defense. He suffered through an illegal confrontation with Annas and an illegal convening and conspiracy of the Sanhedrin. In spite of all that hell and the world tried, they couldn't find one thing He did that was wrong.

What a blessed Savior we have! He is perfect, found to be so at the tribunal of evil men. Who actually was on trial that day were those who accused Jesus. They revealed themselves to be wretched, wicked, sinful, unjust men. Christ, by His very presence, identifies those who side with Satan.

Focusing on the Facts

1. What verse was the Judaic justice system predicated on? Explain it (see p. 94).
2. How did the Jewish people put that verse into practice (see p. 95)?
3. Describe the composition of the great Sanhedrin (see p. 95).

4. How were judges chosen to serve on the Sanhedrin (see p. 95)?

5. What guarantees did the Sanhedrin offer every accused person (see p. 96)?

6. What happened to any false witness once he was caught giving false testimony (see pp. 96-97)?

7. Why was there a delay of three days before executing a convicted criminal (see p. 97)?

8. Who served as the executioners (see p. 97)?

9. Give a synopsis of the procedure that was followed in a typical criminal case heard by the Sanhedrin (see pp. 97-100).

10. In what ways did the Sanhedrin violate proper procedure in the case of Christ (see p. 101)?

11. How many trials did Christ go through? How many phases? Explain (see pp. 101-2).

12. What was the typological significance of Christ's being tied up when He was arrested (see p. 103)?

13. How did Annas violate proper legal procedure in his questioning of Christ (John 18:19-21; see pp. 103-4)?

14. Why did the officer slap Christ (John 18:22; see p. 104)?

15. Describe how Jesus responded to being hit (John 18:23; see pp. 104-5).

16. Who may have been absent from the gathering of the Sanhedrin? Why (Luke 23:50-51; see p. 106)?

17. Where was the trial before Caiaphas and the Sanhedrin held? Why was that illegal (see pp. 106-7)?

18. What did the Sanhedrin have to do first before they could judge Christ (see p. 107)?

19. What was the only way the Sanhedrin could come up with a crime against Christ (Matt. 26:59; see pp. 107-8)?

20. What false testimony was admitted as an accusation against Christ? Explain how it disagreed with what Christ actually said (cf. Matt. 26:60-61; Mark 14:57-58; John 2:19; see p. 108).

21. Why should the testimony of these two witnesses never have been admitted (see pp. 108-9)?

Pondering the Principles

1. The Judaic justice system was designed to protect the rights of the accused. But in the case of Christ, most of—if not all of—His rights were violated by the Sanhedrin. Make a list of as many violations as you can find. How many times have you had your

rights violated? Make a list of those occasions. Compare your two lists. Based on your comparison, who suffered more? The next time your rights are violated, how will you respond?

2. The life and conduct of Joseph of Arimathea is an example to follow. Look up the following verses: Matthew 27:57-60, Mark 15:42-46, Luke 23:50-53, John 19:38. Joseph is usually remembered for his kind deed of obtaining Jesus' body and putting it in his own tomb. But what other things does Scripture say about him? How is he characterized? What was his attitude toward the Sanhedrin's trial of Christ? What would you have done had you been Joseph? There will come a time in every believer's life where he will be called on to take his stand with Christ, even when it means opposing his peers. Are you prepared to do it? Ask God to show you how you might strengthen and prepare yourself for that day.

7

The Illegal, Unjust Trials of Jesus—Part 2

Outline

Introduction
A. The Relevance of the Hour
    1. For Satan
        a) His initial plan
        b) His secondary plan
    2. For God
    3. For evil men
B. The Relentlessness of the Mob
    1. The potent miracles
        a) A miracle of power and judgment
        b) A miracle of kindness and mercy
    2. The possible conclusions

Review
  I. The Illegal, Unjust Confrontation (John 18:12-13, 19-24)
 II. The Illegal, Unjust Convening (Matthew 26:57)
III. The Illegal, Unjust Conspiracy (Matthew 26:59-61)

Lesson
IV. The Illegal, Unjust Condemnation (Matthew 26:62-64)
    A. The Frustration of Caiaphas (v. 62)
        1. Jesus upheld the law
        2. Jesus put the Sanhedrin on trial
    B. The Peace of Christ (v. 63*a*)
    C. The Charge of Blasphemy (v. 63*b*)
        1. Christ's claim to be the Messiah
        2. Christ's claim to be the Son of God
    D. The Prediction of Christ (v. 64)

Introduction

A. The Relevance of the Hour

   1. For Satan

      Jesus told those who came to arrest Him, "This is your hour, and the power of darkness" (Luke 22:53). It was hell's moment to do its deed. When Judas left the upper room before Jesus instituted the Lord's Table, "Satan entered into him" (John 13:27). Satan energized Judas to do his evil deed. No doubt Satan and his demons also energized the high priest, the Sanhedrin, and all those involved in the execution of Jesus Christ.

      a) His initial plan

      Satan was now trying a new approach. Previously he had tried to prevent Christ from going to the cross. Certainly that was his plan in his first temptation of Christ (Matt. 4; Luke 4). Immediately after Jesus was baptized, Satan tried to divert Him from the cross. That may have been his plan in the garden, as our

Lord sweat great drops of blood and agonized in the midst of that temptation. Satan was still trying to do whatever he could to divert Christ from the cross. He knew the cross would provide the salvation for the redeemed of all ages.

b) His secondary plan

Apparently Satan now was resigned to the fact that Jesus was going to the cross—that it was inevitable in the plan of God. So he turned his efforts toward making Christ's death on the cross so final that He could not rise again. That demonstrates both the impotence and inconsistency of Satan—he can't do what he wants to, and he changes his plans frequently. Evil is ultimately inconsistent. That's why it's difficult for us to understand why Satan does what he does. But it appears he had energized the betrayal of Christ, and now the death of Christ. Even after Christ did rise, breaking through Satan's bonds of death, Satan spread lies that He had not risen in an effort to stop the message of the resurrection.

Satan was behind the scenes of Christ's betrayal, arrest, trials, and crucifixion. Jesus said this to the leaders who wanted Him dead: "Ye are of your father the devil. . . . He was a murderer from the beginning. . . . He is a liar, and the father of it" (John 8:44).

2. For God

The arrest and trials of Christ also represent a holy hour—God also is at work. God intends the anger, hatred, and evil of Satan to fit within His own redemptive purpose. Christ could say with Joseph, "Ye thought evil against me, but God meant it unto good" (Gen. 50:20). Whatever latitude Satan has is always within the confines of God's will. So although we know it is the moment of Satan, we also remember that Christ was "being delivered by the determinant counsel and foreknowledge of God" (Acts 2:23). It is a plan that was carried out by hell but had its origin in heaven.

3. For evil men

A third party was involved in the arrest and execution of Christ: evil men. The evil rulers conspired long before to eliminate Jesus Christ. A short time after Jesus raised Lazarus from the dead and a few weeks before Christ's arrest, they met together and said, "This man doeth many miracles" (John 11:47). They knew He did miracles—they were of such significance and frequency that no one could deny them. But this is the conclusion they came to: "If we let him thus alone, all men will believe on him; and the Romans shall come and take away both our place [Temple] and nation" (v. 48). They believed all people would begin to follow Jesus. As the Romans saw the populace moving toward Jesus, they would be worried about a revolution. Then they would react to that by taking away the Jewish leaders' positions, destroying their Temple, and wiping out their nation.

The crowd that had cried, "Hosanna to the Son of David! Blessed is he that cometh in the name of the Lord!" (Matt. 21:9) when He rode into the city on Monday posed a great threat to their security. That's what prompted Caiaphas to say, "Ye know nothing at all, nor consider that it is expedient for us that one man should die for the people, and that the whole nation perish not" (John 11:49-50). John 11:51 says, "This spoke he not of himself; but, being high priest that year, he prophesied that Jesus should die for that nation." Out of a mouth filled with hatred came a prophecy of the substitutionary death of Jesus Christ for the redemption of His people.

In the arrest and trials of Christ, we see the blending of the plot of hell, the plan of God, and the hatred of evil Christ-rejecting people. But understand this: although it is the plan of God, that in no way lessens the evil of hell's conspiracy and the men who carried it out. Their guilt is not mitigated. It was the plan of God, but they willed to do it. They chose to be the compatriots of hell by their own volition.

B. The Relentlessness of the Mob

We pick up the scene in the Garden of Gethsemane where the mob took Jesus captive. It is tragic in that there is a certain relentlessness about their approach. They came to take Jesus Christ, the King of glory and Son of God, with a relentlessness that's staggering. Let me show you what I mean.

1. The potent miracles

    a) A miracle of power and judgment

    When Jesus went to meet the mob in the garden, the entire crowd of nearly one thousand fell down on the ground at the moment He identified Himself (John 18:6). The very power of His person knocked them to the ground as if they'd been hit by a celestial hammer. They had just been exposed to the power and judgment of the Son of the living God. Now you would think that any thoughtful person would say to himself, *This is not just another man.* They all should have understood such a miracle of power and judgment as a warning to examine who He was. But it found absolutely no response in their hard hearts. The terrifying power that knocked them to the ground brought about no thought of the deity or lordship of Jesus Christ. As clear as it was, they bypassed that warning sign.

    b) A miracle of kindness and mercy

    A little later, Peter sliced off the ear of Malchus, the servant of the high priest (John 18:10). Jesus responded to Peter's attack by calling a stop to it and then instantaneously creating a new ear for Malchus (Luke 22:51). That was a miracle not of power and judgment but of kindness and mercy. If you were a part of that mob and had just seen a miracle like that, you would most likely say to yourself, *Certainly one with such incredible creative power is someone to reckon with. We'd better stop and examine who this is.* But, again, they bypassed another signpost.

2. The possible conclusions

There are only two possible conclusions: one, they believed He wasn't the Messiah. But if they believed He wasn't the Messiah, they would have tried to prove He wasn't. The other conclusion is that they were afraid He was the Messiah—they didn't want to go through an examination because they were afraid of what they would discover. They simply wanted Him out of the way. They didn't want to know if He was their Messiah or not. Why? Because they were locked into their own false religion, with the accompanying self-righteous lifestyle, power, and prestige. Jesus' true holiness, purity, and power threatened them, and they were afraid to find out the truth. If they found Him to be the Messiah, His words had already damned them. So rather than find out the truth, they wanted to eliminate Him. If at any moment they believed He might not be the Messiah, I believe they would have conducted a more thorough investigation.

The relentlessness of the religious leaders to kill Christ went beyond reality and His miracles. After the resurrection of Lazarus they said, "This man doeth many miracles" (John 11:47). They couldn't deny that; they just didn't want to face what it meant, which was their own judgment.

Mark 14:51-52 tells us a young man who had been observing the arrest was grabbed by some men in the crowd. They ripped off his outer garment, and he ran away wearing only his undergarment. The narrative of that event is one way Scripture shows us the violence of the scene. This was an agitated mob. Here they grabbed someone they weren't interested in arresting, and they ripped off his clothes in their effort to seize him. This frenzied mob took Jesus captive and led Him away "as a lamb to the slaughter" (Isa. 53:7).

Review

Before the rulers had Jesus executed, they had a trial—although unjust and illegal. Such a trial was unusual for a people committed to a great system of justice. Their supreme court was the Sanhedrin (see pp. 95-97). It was built on the premise that every defendant in a trial was entitled to three things: a public trial, an opportunity to present a defense, and a conviction confirmed by at least two or three witnesses.

The Sanhedrin also followed some important laws. Any false witness would pay the same penalty as the one he witnessed against. They could not prosecute the accused; they could only try him. No court could convene at night or in any other place except the Judgment Hall. No hearing could convene in the late afternoon, lest justice be hurried to a hasty and wrongful conclusion. No convicted criminal could be executed the same day he was tried. A one-day interval was required. No execution could be held on a feast day or the day before. All the votes were carefully counted. And no one could incriminate himself by giving testimony against himself.

The Jewish leaders violated every one of those safeguards. They never gave Jesus a public trial; they held it privately. They didn't allow Him to make a defense—no witnesses spoke on His behalf. They couldn't find two or more witnesses to convict Him of anything. They actually bribed some false witnesses, which was contrary to their efforts of discouraging false witnesses through severe punishment. They were not allowed to prosecute an individual, yet they did that. There was no prior prosecution because there was no crime. They met in the middle of the night. They sentenced and executed Him the same day. The trial took place on a feast day. They met outside the Hall of Judgment. And they never counted the votes.

I. THE ILLEGAL, UNJUST CONFRONTATION (John 18:12-13, 19-24; see pp. 102-5)

II. THE ILLEGAL, UNJUST CONVENING (Matthew 26:57; see pp. 105-7)

III. THE ILLEGAL, UNJUST CONSPIRACY (Matthew 26:59-61; see pp. 107-9)

Since the leaders couldn't come up with any accusation, they brought in false witnesses. They found two, but even their testimonies didn't agree. The reason they couldn't bring an accusation is that Christ never did anything wrong. He was God in human flesh. He was absolutely impeccable. The leaders had decided to put Christ to death (v. 59), and now they needed to find a reason. But the testimony of the two witnesses was useless, since it was based on something Jesus said. There was no way they could require death for that. The inability to find a crime frustrated Caiaphas.

Lesson

IV. THE ILLEGAL, UNJUST CONDEMNATION (Matthew 26:62-64)

The religious leaders were in a hurry to convict Jesus before dawn—before people began to mill around. They were afraid of His popularity with them and of what might happen if the people found out what they were trying to do. They wanted to finish the trial so they could celebrate the Passover with unbloodied hands.

A. The Frustration of Caiaphas (v. 62)

"The high priest arose and said unto him [Jesus], Answereth thou nothing? What is it which these witness against thee?"

Frustration reached its apex in Caiaphas. False witnesses paraded before the Sanhedrin, none of whom could concoct believable lies about Jesus. While that went on, Jesus stood staring into the eyes of Caiaphas with a gaze that must have burned his soul. Never did He say a word. The frustration and hatred of Caiaphas and the rest of the Sanhedrin mounted as they waited for Jesus to say something they could attack and thus release their passion. Even after the two witnesses presented their twisted testimony, Jesus still said nothing. The air was filled with lies and inconsistencies. The mockery of justice dominated the scene. The Sanhedrin became even more desperate for Jesus to say something so they could twist that and make it the new issue. Yet all they could hear up to this point was the echo of their own stupidity and anger.

1. Jesus upheld the law

Jesus said nothing because there was nothing to say. If they weren't going to uphold Jewish law, He would. And one of those laws said that a man could not incriminate himself. Maimonides, a Jewish medieval scholar, said that the law does not permit the death penalty as a sentence for a sinner by his own confession. That had always been central to Jewish law. Jesus had nothing to say, and the law made provision for Him to stay silent. He had to be accused by others and proved guilty by them. There was nothing to say anyway, because there had been no true testimony, only contrary statements about something He was supposed to have said. So Jesus stood before the Sanhedrin and allowed the echo of their words to ring through the hall of Caiaphas's house.

2. Jesus put the Sanhedrin on trial

The contrast between the calmness of Christ and the fury of Caiaphas is striking. When anyone looks at this scene objectively, he won't see Jesus on trial, he'll see the Sanhedrin put to task. It's clear who Christ was. There was no need for retaliation, vindication, or self-defense. Jesus stood before Caiaphas, resolutely headed for the cross. He knew it was His hour to die for the sins of the world.

B. The Peace of Christ (v. 63a)

"Jesus held His peace."

That's another way of saying he kept silent. Caiaphas must have continually badgered Him to say something, but He did not. The prophet Isaiah said, "As a sheep before her shearers is dumb, so he openeth not his mouth" (Isa. 53:7).

C. The Charge of Blasphemy (v. 63b)

"The high priest answered and said unto him, I adjure thee by the living God, that thou tell us whether thou be the Christ, the Son of God."

Caiaphas called on Jesus to make the most sacred oath a Jew could ever speak—to answer the question truthfully as a vow before the living God. It was an oath to the God of truth who punishes liars. Here Caiaphas wanted Jesus to claim to be the Son of God, a claim to deity. That was considered a blasphemous claim for a human to make, so he was trying to get Jesus to blaspheme. If He was successful, they would have their reason for executing Him. Leviticus 24:16 says, "He who blasphemeth the name of the Lord, he shall surely be put to death." So the crime they attached to Christ was that He said He was God. But that wasn't a crime because it happened to be the truth. Jesus was not executed for saying He was God but for being God.

1. Christ's claim to be the Messiah

Jesus had previously claimed to be the Messiah. After reading a messianic prophecy from the book of Isaiah in the synagogue in Nazareth, He said, "This day is this scripture fulfilled in your ears" (Luke 4:21). That was a claim to be the Messiah. On a different occasion Christ met a woman of Samaria. She said to Him, "I know that Messiah cometh" (John 4:25). He replied, "I that speak unto thee am he" (v. 26). He claimed overtly to be the promised Messiah—the deliverer and Savior of Israel. That was something He never denied; He always affirmed it. That Caiaphas asked Him if He was the Christ indicated that he knew Jesus claimed to be the Messiah. When Christ rode into the city of Jerusalem, "the multitudes that went before, and that followed, cried, saying, Hosanna to the Son of David! Blessed is he that cometh in the name of the Lord!" (Matt. 21:9). Those names were all messianic titles. It was perfectly clear that Jesus had claimed to be the Messiah.

However, Jesus never flaunted the fact that He was the Messiah. He didn't want to cause problems outside the proper plan of God. Although He claimed to be the

Messiah in no uncertain terms, He told His disciples to "tell no man that he was Jesus, the Christ" (Matt. 16:20). He avoided the danger and the threats. He avoided what might happen if people became upset at such a claim. So while He claimed to be the Messiah, He did so cautiously.

2. Christ's claim to be the Son of God

The Sanhedrin knew Jesus had also claimed to be the Son of God. That's why Caiaphas asked Him if He was the Son of God. But what did Caiaphas mean? Did he believe Christ claimed to be just another offspring of God or another creature God made? No, he meant deity. Why else would they charge Christ with blasphemy? If He was a son of God like everyone is a child of God in that He loved God and was created by Him, then affirming so wouldn't be blasphemous. But Caiaphas knew what Christ meant. When Jesus said He was the Son of God, He meant He was equal with God, for a son is of the same essence and nature as his father. Jesus had said continually, "I and my Father are one" (John 10:30). Throughout the gospel of John, Jesus claims to be the Son of God. Even John 19:7 says, "The Jews answered him [Pilate], We have a law, and by our law he ought to die, because he made himself the Son of God."

Caiaphas knew Jesus claimed to be the Messiah—the anointed One, the coming King and ruler of Israel. As such He was a threat to his rule and priesthood. And He claimed to be the Son of the living God, a claim no one could make even in a cautious way without its spreading like wildfire. Caiaphas wanted to hear those claims from Jesus' own mouth so he would have reason to execute Him.

D. The Prediction of Christ (v. 64)

1. Christ's present reaffirmation (v. 64a)

"Jesus saith unto him, Thou hast said."

Mark 14:62 adds that Jesus also said, "I am." Jesus took the oath of the living God and affirmed that He was the anointed Messiah and the Son of God. This was not a time for Him to be cautious; it was time for Him to die. So Christ was frank with the Sanhedrin about His claims.

2. Christ's future role (v. 64b)

"Nevertheless, I say unto you, Hereafter shall ye see the Son of man sitting on the right hand of power, and coming in the clouds of heaven."

a) His exaltation

That is a quote from Daniel 7:13-14, a great messianic prophecy. What an amazing claim! Jesus affirmed before the Sanhedrin that He was God, and that soon they would see Him exalted to the right hand of God and coming in the clouds of heaven. One day He will return to earth as Judge and King to establish His eternal kingdom. Jesus claimed that He was the one Daniel spoke of.

b) His judgment

When Jesus said, "Hereafter shall ye see," He was informing Caiaphas that he would see Him again on that day. Caiaphas would see Christ at the great white throne when He calls out of the graves all those who rejected Him and His Father (John 5:25-29). Jesus will then become Caiaphas's eternal Judge. Jesus referred to Himself as "Son of man" in Matthew 26:64 because that's the phrase Daniel used in his prophecy. That title also was Christ's most common name for Himself. He is the Son of man and the Son of God—fully man and fully God.

In the eyes of the Sanhedrin, Jesus condemned Himself by His own words. But that alone was unjust and illegal. They claimed He incriminated Himself with His blasphemy—that He had the audacity to claim to be the fulfillment of Daniel 7:13-14. Jesus was right—He was equal with God and would be elevated to God's right hand. Hebrews 1:3 calls Jesus Christ "the express image of [God's] person." It also says that when He had finished His work, He "sat down on the right hand of the Majesty on high." Matthew 24:30 says that one day the Son of man will come "in the clouds of heaven with power and great glory." Jesus affirmed that His death would usher Him into God's presence for His coronation. He would then remain at the right hand [a symbol of power] of God as King and Ruler. But one day soon He will return in glory. Those who stood in judgment against Christ will some day be judged by Him.

V. THE ILLEGAL, UNJUST CONCLUSION (Matthew 26:65-66)

A. The Accusation of Blasphemy (v. 65)

"The high priest tore his clothes, saying, He hath spoken blasphemy! What further need have we of witnesses? Behold, now ye have heard his blasphemy."

1. Avoiding truth

Was Jesus' claim to be God blasphemy? No, because what He said was true. But the high priest didn't want to know the truth. Jesus said, "If I do not the works of my Father, believe me not. But if I do, though ye believe not me, believe the works" (John 10:37-38). The rulers knew He had performed miracles. They knew He had raised Lazarus from the dead. But they didn't want to know the truth. They closed their minds to it out of fear. People today reject Christ because they are afraid to examine the issues. They know that if they do their lives will be overturned and exposed for what they are. They would rather go to hell blind than to find the truth.

2. Applying theatrics

Caiaphas did what a high priest had the right to do when God was dishonored—tear his garments (Lev. 21:10). But in Caiaphas's case it was mere theatrics. He wasn't concerned about God's name; he was happy because Jesus could now be executed. But he put on a show to appear grieved. Such histrionics were typical among ancient peoples. Whenever they wanted to express grief, distress, or intense emotion, they would rip their clothes. It may well have been that members of the Sanhedrin wore garments that had been sewed many times because they had performed those kind of theatrics before. Caiaphas ripped his clothes to appear as if he were defending the holiness of God, but inwardly he was rejoicing at the prospect of getting rid of Jesus Christ.

When Caiaphas said "What further need have we of witnesses?" he was effectively putting an end to the trial. No one was brought in to testify for Jesus. No evidence was presented. There was no proof that Jesus was not the Son of God.

B. The Violation of Protocol (v. 66)

"What think ye? They answered and said, He is guilty of death."

That procedure was not according to judicial protocol. No scribe was recording the votes. There was no pause between each vote so each judge could weigh the seriousness of his decision. It was nothing more than a rabble. They were a mad mob, screaming for His blood. There was no justice. Mark 14:64 says their vote was unanimous. The usual careful vote was thrown out.

VI. THE ILLEGAL, UNJUST CONDUCT (Matthew 26:67-68)

"Then they spat in his face, and buffeted him; and others smote him with the palms of their hands, saying, Prophesy unto us, thou Christ, Who smote thee?"

A. The Contempt of the Aristocracy

The Jewish aristocracy—the high priest, elders, chief priests, and scribes—abused Christ. They were the leaders of the nation, and they constituted the supreme court. To show you how utterly possessed they were by the demons of hell, Luke 22:65 says, "Many other things blasphemously spoke they against him." The blasphemer wasn't Jesus; the Sanhedrin itself was full of blasphemers. Jesus claimed to be God. That wasn't blasphemy; it was truth. But spitting in the face of God is blasphemy—blasphemy of an inconceivable kind. Luke 22:64 adds, "When they had blindfolded Him, they struck him on the face, and asked him, saying, Prophesy, who is it that smote thee?" That's frightening, considering whom they were dealing with!

1. They spit on Him

A supreme sign of contempt in Jewish culture was to spit on someone or something (Num. 12:14). A tomb in the Valley of Kidron is known as Absalom's tomb. The Jewish people have long hated the memory of Absalom because he was a traitor to his father, David. He even tried to take his father's life. To this day, when anyone who is faithful to Judaistic tradition walks by Absalom's tomb, he will spit on it. Spit is a symbol of disdain, and the Sanhedrin spit in the face of God.

2. They struck Him

The judges also buffeted (Gk., *kolaphizō*), or hit, Christ with their fists. They punched Him as if He were a punching bag. Others slapped Him with the palms of their hands. They ridiculed and mocked His supposed deity by asking Him to prophesy who hit Him. Mark 14:65 adds, "The guards did strike him with the palms of their hands." Even the Temple police took part in the mockery.

B. The Compassion of Christ

The nation of Israel was rotten—a rotten carcass waiting to be eaten by the Roman eagle. The representatives of the nation had abandoned all sense of virtue, righteousness, and holiness. They spat on the One who taught them to love their enemies. He who smiled at the approach of a child, who beamed when a sinner became a saint, and who mirrored the loving heart of God was prepared to die on the cross for the very people who spit on Him.

The religious leaders framed their own Messiah. They pretended to know God, but when God came to them, they spit on Him. They were far from the truth, intent on protecting their power, prestige, and position. Anyone who rejects Jesus Christ today stands with those religious phonies. Jesus said, "He that is not with me is against me" (Matt. 12:30).

Conclusion

Ironically, those who misjudge Jesus will be rightly judged by Him one day. The tables will be turned. The judges who tried Christ were nothing more than criminals, and they will be justly condemned. The One wrongly accused will one day become the Judge. The damning sin is the sin of unbelief, which encompasses pride, impenitence, independence, and self-sufficiency. It is the sin of thinking you can be right with God without Christ.

As I look at the scene of Christ before the Sanhedrin, I'm overwhelmed by God's grace. I deserve the trial, the sentence, the condemnation, and the execution Christ endured for me. It is God who should spit in my face, punch and slap me around, and then execute me. But Christ took my place.

I was once a captive of Satan, but Christ became a captive so I might be set free. I was once a forsaken outcast—apart from the fellowship of God—but Christ became forsaken and an outcast for me. He was forsaken by all His own that I might be made forever a member of the family of God. I was once denied compassion and sympathy, but Jesus went to a death without compassion for me. Now He is my sympathetic high priest who understands and cares for me. I was once accursed, but Jesus became accursed for me. I was once a false witness who denied the truth about Christ, but Christ endured false witnesses to make me His own. Now no one can ever bring an accusation against me that will make me lose my salvation. I saw Jesus remain silent for me. Shouldn't I fill my mouth with praise for Him? I was dead, but Jesus died that I might live.

Focusing on the Facts

1. What had Satan been trying to do to Christ throughout His earthly ministry (see p. 114-15)?
2. What new approach did Satan take once Christ's death was imminent (see p. 115)?
3. Explain why the arrest and trials of Christ represent a holy hour (see p. 115).

4. Explain the conspiracy of the religious leaders in John 11:47-51. What motivated the conspiracy (see pp. 115-16)?

5. What kind of response should the mob have displayed after being knocked to the ground by Christ? How should they have responded when He healed Malchus's ear (see p. 117)?

6. What were the people in the crowd unwilling to face even after witnessing Christ's miracles (see pp. 117-18)?

7. Why was the Sanhedrin in a hurry to convict Christ before dawn (see p. 120)?

8. What did Jesus uphold by remaining silent before the Sanhedrin (see pp. 120-21)?

9. Why did Caiaphas ask Jesus if He was the Son of God (see pp. 121-22)?

10. Cite some instances when Christ claimed to be the Messiah (see p. 122).

11. What did Caiaphas understand Jesus to mean by His claim to be the Son of God (see p. 123)?

12. After affirming to Caiaphas that He was the Son of God, what did Jesus tell him in the rest of His statement? Explain (Matt. 26:64; see p. 124).

13. Why did the religious leaders avoid examining Christ's works (see p. 125)?

14. Why did Caiaphas tear his clothes? How did he really feel (see p. 125)?

15. Why did the members of the court spit on Jesus after convicting Him (see p. 127)?

Pondering the Principles

1. In Genesis 50:20 Joseph said, "Ye thought evil against me, but God meant it unto good." We have already seen how God used the wickedness of the Jewish leaders to accomplish redemption for all men (Acts 2:23). Have there been occasions in your life when God turned something evil into good? What were the circumstances? Thank God for His plan for your life. As you encounter future circumstances that appear to be bad, remember the times when God turned bad circumstances to your benefit.

2. Christ often claimed to be both the Messiah and the Son of God. As a long-term study, read through the gospels. Each time you read a reference to Jesus' claiming to be either the Messiah or

the Son of God record it. Also record the context of events in which He made the claim. When you are finished, study your list. What conclusions can you make that apply to you personally? How might you use what you have discovered in developing a strategy for proclaiming the deity of Christ to the unsaved?

8

The Restoration of a Sinning Saint

Outline

Introduction

Lesson
  I. The Sinner's Boast (vv. 31-33)
     A. The Prediction of the Disciples' Defection (vv. 31-32)
     B. The Display of Peter's Self-Confidence (v. 33)
 II. The Sinner's Defiance (vv. 34-35)
     A. Christ's Prediction of Peter's Denials (v. 34)
     B. Peter's Protest over Christ's Prediction (v. 35)
III. The Sinner's Indifference (vv. 36-41)
 IV. The Sinner's Impulsiveness (vv. 51-52)
     A. Peter's Act of Violence (v. 51)
     B. Christ's Appeal for Non-Violence (vv. 52-54)
  V. The Sinner's Collapse (vv. 58, 69-74)
     A. The Context of Peter's Denials (v. 58)
        1. He followed at a distance (v. 58a)
           a) John's connections
           b) The lesson's purpose
        2. He exposed himself to sin (v. 58b)
     B. The Circumstances of Peter's Denials (vv. 69-74)
        1. The first occasion (vv. 69-70)
           a) A slave girl's accusation (v. 69)
           b) Peter's denial (v. 70)
              (1) His faulty preparation
              (2) His faulty confidence
        2. The second occasion (vv. 71-72)
           a) Peter's disappearance (v. 71a)
           b) Another slave girl's accusation (v. 71b)
           c) Peter's denial (v. 72)

Introduction

What is the single greatest gift God could give? The obvious answer is forgiveness of sin. There can be no salvation, no relationship with God, and no entrance into heaven unless one's sins are forgiven. We know no usefulness to the Lord or relief from the guilt of sin without the forgiveness of sin.

Such was the experience of Peter. The depth of his sin gave God opportunity to reveal the extent of His forgiveness. Peter, who fell so deeply, was soon restored to become the leading spokesman and great leader of the early church. His is a hopeful record, a thrilling and encouraging story for all who are sinners saved by God's grace.

To better understand Matthew 26:58, 69-75, we need to see the background of Peter's denial woven through the tapestry of the arrest and trial of Christ. His denial did not happen spontaneously. To discover why it happened let's look back at the sequence of events that led to his denials.

Lesson

I. THE SINNER'S BOAST (vv. 31-33)

Matthew 26:30 tells us that the Lord and the eleven disciples had sung a hymn in the upper room and then left for the

Mount of Olives. Judas had already left to work out the details of his betrayal of Christ.

A. The Prediction of the Disciples' Defection (vv. 31-32)

> "Then saith Jesus unto them, All ye shall be offended because of me this night; for it is written, I will smite the shepherd, and the sheep of the flock shall be scattered abroad. But after I am raised up again, I will go before you into Galilee."

After predicting the defection of the disciples, Jesus then predicts His own resurrection and His regathering of the scattered disciples. They would forsake Him at the moment of His greatest trial, which was the struggle He endured throughout His arrest, trials, and crucifixion. But that was not to be the end of the story, because He would rise from the grave and regather the disciples.

B. The Display of Peter's Self-Confidence (v. 33)

> "Peter answered and said unto him, Though all men shall be offended because of thee, yet will I never be offended."

Rather loudly and vehemently Peter protested the Lord's prediction of the disciples' defection. Because of his love for Christ, he believed he was invincible. He couldn't accept Jesus' prediction. He believed he was spiritually mature, that his priorities were cast in concrete—thus making him invulnerable to the onslaughts of Satan, the world, and the flesh. He couldn't imagine any circumstance that would cause him to defect and deny the Lord Jesus Christ. He didn't believe there could be any pressure that great. So boastfully he told the Lord that He was wrong. It takes a big ego to contradict the word of the living God, and Peter had one.

II. THE SINNER'S DEFIANCE (vv. 34-35)

A. Christ's Prediction of Peter's Denials (v. 34)

> "Jesus said unto him, Verily I say unto thee that this night, before the cock crows, thou shalt deny me thrice."

Jesus made an even stronger prediction, and this time He directed it at Peter. He told him that not only would he defect but that he would go one step further and actually deny Him three times.

B. Peter's Protest over Christ's Prediction (v. 35)

"Peter said unto him, Though I should die with thee, yet will I not deny thee. Likewise also said all the disciples."

When the Lord predicts Peter's denial in verse 34, Matthew uses a strong Greek verb that means "to deny completely." Peter couldn't accept that. Mark 14:31 says Peter vehemently protested Christ's prediction. When Peter said he was willing to die, he was speaking courageously. But such a boast was in defiance of Christ's word.

III. THE SINNER'S INDIFFERENCE (vv. 36-41)

"Then cometh Jesus with them unto a place called Gethsemane, and saith unto the disciples, Sit here, while I go and pray yonder. And he took with him Peter and the two sons of Zebedee, and began to be sorrowful and very depressed. Then saith he unto them, My soul is exceedingly sorrowful, even unto death; tarry here, and watch with me. And he went a little further, and fell on his face, and prayed, saying, O my Father, if it be possible, let this cup pass from me; nevertheless, not as I will, but as thou wilt. And he cometh unto the disciples, and findeth them asleep; and he saith unto Peter, What, could ye not watch with me one hour? Watch and pray, that ye enter not into temptation; the spirit indeed is willing, but the flesh is weak."

We know Peter's spirit was willing, and all the other disciples affirmed they also were willing to die for the Lord. But their flesh wasn't able to let them do it. They should have been praying, but the smug, boastful, self-confident disciples didn't pray because they believed they didn't need to. They felt invincible and invulnerable. Instead of being alert to the coming hour of darkness, they went to sleep. They had made their vow. They believed they'd remain faithful to Jesus based on their emotions and affection for Him and their verbal commitment.

IV. THE SINNER'S IMPULSIVENESS (vv. 51-52)

A. Peter's Act of Violence (v. 51)

"Behold, one of those who were with Jesus stretched out his hand, and drew his sword, and struck a servant of the high priest's, and smote off his ear."

The first person Peter attacked was Malchus, the servant of the high priest. Peter probably tried to cut off his head and missed, cutting off his ear instead. That wasn't what Jesus wanted. Peter had forgotten the times Jesus said He must go to Jerusalem, be taken captive, lay down His life, and rise again (Matt. 16:21; 17:22-23; 20:18-19). Peter also protested that initial prediction. That's when the Lord rebuked him for letting Satan speak through him (v. 23).

B. Christ's Appeal for Non-Violence (vv. 52-54)

"Then said Jesus unto him, Put up again thy sword into its place; for all they that take the sword shall perish with the sword. Thinkest thou that I cannot now pray to my Father, and he shall presently give me more than twelve legions of angels? But how, then, shall the scriptures be fulfilled, that thus it must be?"

Peter was out of alignment with God's plan. He displayed courage, but it was misguided. He was so in defiance of what the Lord said and so zealous of his own plan that he acted impulsively, completely at odds with the plan of God. He wanted to show Jesus and the disciples that he was as courageous as he claimed to be.

V. THE SINNER'S COLLAPSE (vv. 58, 69-74)

John 18:12 tells us that before the soldiers took Jesus to the high priest, they took Him to Annas, a former high priest. John 18:19-24 describes the scene before Annas, whereas Matthew doesn't refer to it. In verse 57 Matthew says the soldiers brought Jesus to Caiaphas.

Does John 18:12 Contradict Matthew 26:57?

It may initially appear that John 18:12 contradicts Matthew 26:57, but it does not. The high priest lived in a palatial home in the city of Jerusalem somewhere near the Temple. In those days it was common for families to share the same home. That was no doubt the case with Annas and Caiaphas. Annas had served previously as the high priest, but he was deposed by the Romans because he was amassing too much power, and he became a threat to them. One of those who replaced him was Caiaphas, the son-in-law of Annas. It was natural for Annas and Caiaphas to occupy the same home, because they were related. Thus when Jesus was led to the home of Caiaphas, where the Sanhedrin was assembling, it was also the home of Annas. There is no conflict. That Jesus was led away to Caiaphas is consistent with His being led away to Annas. No doubt Annas occupied one wing of the house and Caiaphas the other.

Homes in those days were constructed in such a way that they did not face the street. The only thing visible from the street other than the walls of the house was a great gate, which was typical of palatial homes owned by wealthy people. The high priests had become wealthy through the corruption they had organized in the Temple. The gate of the house opened up into a corridor that led to a huge courtyard. The house surrounded the courtyard, and all the rooms on all floors looked out into the courtyard.

One section of this house belonged to Annas; the other belonged to Caiaphas. When Jesus was led to the home of Caiaphas, He was taken to Annas's wing first. Later on He was transferred to the part of the house occupied by Caiaphas. When Matthew says, "They that had laid hold on Jesus led him away to Caiaphas, the high priest, where the scribes and the elders were assembled" (Matt. 26:57), he was referring to the very place where Jesus would face Annas.

Jesus faced Annas first, and then He was taken to Caiaphas and the Sanhedrin for the second phase of the three-part Jewish trial. The third phase occurred just after dawn as the Sanhedrin attempted to legalize their illegal decision of the previous night.

Peter's denials all occurred in the courtyard of the high priest's house. John 18:25-27 indicates that his first denial occurred while Jesus was with Annas.

A. The Context of Peter's Denials (v. 58)

1. He followed at a distance (v. 58*a*)

"Peter followed him afar off unto the high priest's court."

Although all the disciples fled when Jesus was taken prisoner, Peter couldn't stay away. He was pulled along by his love for the Lord. But he followed Christ at a distance. Peter wasn't brave enough to come close.

a) John's connections

Peter wasn't alone. According to John 18:15, another disciple accompanied him. Most likely this other disciple was John, who was known to the high priest. We don't know the circumstances of that relationship, but it would explain what gave Peter and John entrance into the high priest's house.

John and Peter were getting in over their heads by following the Lord—at least we're sure Peter was. We can't be sure about what happened to John. Scripture says nothing about what happened after he went into the house, but we do know he didn't deny the Lord.

By himself, Peter couldn't get in the house because he didn't know anyone who could invite him. Apparently John rectified the situation by talking the girl who watched the door into letting Peter in (John 18:16). In a sense, John unwittingly contributed to Peter's denial of Christ. After this scene John disappears from the narrative of the text. Our focus is on Peter. John's part was to gain access for Peter, and in that way he was a part of the unfolding prediction of Christ.

b) The lesson's purpose

Why would Christ predict that Peter would deny Him and then plan out the events so he could? Because Christ wanted to teach us all profound lessons about spiritual unpreparedness and the restoration of sinning saints. Those are the kinds of lessons we should rejoice to learn.

2. He exposed himself to sin (v. 58*b*)

"[Peter] went in, and sat with the guards, to see the end."

Peter sat with the Temple police (Gk., *hupēretēs*). No doubt the Roman soldiers had already returned to Fort Antonia. They had done their duty by capturing Jesus and taking Him to the place of trial.

According to verse 58, Peter wanted to see the outcome of Christ's trial. But he should have known what the outcome would be; the Lord had told him enough times previously. He simply didn't listen well. Peter couldn't walk away and not know what happened to Christ. His love for the Lord may have been weak, but it was real. He entered the lions' den and totally ignored Christ's prediction of his denials.

As Peter sat by the fire, the Lord was inside before Annas. Perhaps Peter was even able to see Him. A fire was burning because it was a cool night. Many members of the Sanhedrin would have been bustling about as they began to gather for their part in the trial. In addition, house servants and dignitaries that made up the group of people surrounding the high priest would also have been present.

The time was near 1:00 A.M., and the trial would last about two hours. It was in that two-hour span that Peter would hit rock bottom. Peter sat with the soldiers warming himself, trying to lose himself in the crowd. He wanted to stay close enough to find out what was going to happen to Christ but not so close that he would be exposed.

B. The Circumstances of Peter's Denials (vv. 69-74)

  1. The first occasion (vv. 69-70)

    a) A slave girl's accusation (v. 69)

      "Peter sat outside in the court, and a maid came unto him, saying, Thou also wast with Jesus of Galilee."

      Mark 14:66 says she was "one of the maids of the high priest." John 18:17 says she was "the maid that kept the door." Mark 14:67 says she identified the Lord as "Jesus of Nazareth." Jesus' skeptics loved to refer to Him as a Nazarene or Galilean because they were terms of derision. The proud citizens of Jerusalem looked down on people from Galilee. This doorkeeper might have gained her information about Peter because she knew John, whom she knew as a follower of Jesus. She followed Peter and announced her discovery, perhaps to impress the guards sitting around the fire.

      This scene in the courtyard is natural—it is a crowd scene. What we read in the narrative is only a portion of the dialogue that probably occurred. For example, the maid said, "Thou also wast with Jesus of Galilee" (Matt. 26:69). But we can be certain she couldn't say that without capturing the attention of the soldiers and other people first. To make her point she probably identified Peter as one of the followers of Jesus in two or three different ways, which is confirmed in the different gospel accounts of this scene. When we see slight variations in what she said from one gospel to another we shouldn't be surprised.

    b) Peter's denial (v. 70)

      "He denied it before them all, saying, I know not what thou sayest."

      Peter did not address his denial to the maiden but to those near the fire. Mark 14:68 records Peter as saying, "I know not [Him]." In John 18:17 Peter says, "I am not." He probably said, "I am not. I don't know Him. You don't know what you're saying." That would have been a natural response. We don't want to become overprotective of the exactness of each book, otherwise we'll invent contradictions that aren't there. Each author picked each detail as the Holy Spirit led him. All four gospels together give us a more complete picture. The scene was natural—Peter denied knowing Christ with several statements, perhaps with even more than are recorded.

(1) His faulty preparation

> The question we must answer is how could Peter deny Christ, especially after saying he was ready to die for Him? Peter was Christ's main man—the leader of the Twelve. He had been given the keys to the kingdom by the King Himself. Peter was a privileged man. He had witnessed Christ's miraculous power and had been given the same power to heal diseases (Matt. 10:8). He was not some new convert or simply a personal acquaintance of Christ. So why did Peter deny Him?

Dropping Our Guard

I believe Peter was prepared for a big test. If the Lord suddenly sent for him and said, "Come into My trial and speak on My behalf," Peter may have stood by the Lord and felt invincible, as he did in the garden (John 18:10). He may have been ready for the opportunity to be a speaker for the Lord. But he wasn't prepared for the little, unexpected test. I'm afraid we're all like that. We prepare well for our Bible study or to communicate Christ in certain situations. We may be able to anticipate future challenging situations and prepare ourselves to meet them. But while we're prepared for those situations, we often are suddenly hit with a situation we never expected. That knocks us off our guard, and we deny Christ. Peter was prepared for the big test; it was the little one that trapped him. Since the Lord wasn't at his side, he became afraid and denied having had any relationship with Jesus at all.

Peter's response is reminiscent of Elijah's. After slaughtering 450 false priests of Baal (1 Kings 18:40), Elijah fled from Jezebel once he heard about her threat to kill him (1 Kings 19:2-3). How could he go from such heights of victory to such depths of defeat? Peter had reached similar heights. He had just come out of the upper room where he had seen Jesus close out the Old Covenant and initiate the New Covenant. He had heard Jesus promise them things never before heard by any human being, or by any since. He had seen the Lord knock down a thousand people with a word. He had seen Jesus restore a severed ear. On top of that, Peter had briefly walked on water (Matt. 14:29) and seen Jesus raise Lazarus from the dead (John 11:44).

(2) His faulty confidence

Peter is a living illustration of the following principle: "Let him that thinketh he standeth take heed lest he fall" (1 Cor. 10:12). His confidence became his undoing. A doormaid was able to fell the chief of the Twelve. Gone were his heroic protestations to Jesus. Gone was his courage. Jesus had snatched a sword from his hand, and now a girl has snatched his character from his heart. He was revealed as an arrogant coward, unable to confess his heavenly Lord, cringing in denial. He was afraid of being arrested. His instinct for self-preservation took over, and he denied what he knew to be true.

Revealing Character

Our involuntary responses reveal our character, not our planned responses. Your character isn't manifested by what you are prepared to do, but by what you're not prepared for and how you react to it. To some extent we can plan for certain experiences we know might be trying. But the experiences that catch us off guard are those that reveal our weaknesses and show us for what we really are. Peter was caught off guard. He wasn't prepared for his test. His involuntary reaction revealed his character to be weak and sinful. A new character flaw it wasn't, issuing from a strong ego, an unwillingness to listen to the word of the Lord, a failure to pray, a tendency to act on impulse, and a disregard for the plan of God. Peter was on his own, and on his own he was weak, just like anyone else.

2. The second occasion (vv. 71-72)

a) Peter's disappearance (v. 71a)

"When he was gone out into the porch."

Luke 22:58 says that "after a little while" he went out to the porch. After denying the Lord by the fire, Peter couldn't leave immediately, or it would look like he was lying. So he hung around for a little while. But then he moved away from the fire inconspicuously. Verse 71 says he went into the porch, which was the corridor that led out to the gate of the house. It's quite possible that Peter was attempting to leave, but I don't believe so. In that courtyard were two places to keep warm on a cold night—by the fire or in the corridor away from the wind. So Peter went to the corridor to keep warm but also to hide because it would be darker there. He wouldn't be exposed to either the moonlight or firelight.

Mark 14:68 says, "He went out into the porch; and the cock crowed." He denied the Lord once, and the cock crowed once. After two more denials the cock would crow a second time.

b) Another slave girl's accusation (v. 71b)

"Another maid [Gk., allē, another girl of the same kind] saw him, and said unto them that were there, This fellow was also with Jesus of Nazareth."

Again Peter was exposed. He couldn't avoid it. Matthew tells us the maid was another servant girl. Luke 22:58 indicates that at this time a man also confronted him. Again, we get a more complete picture when we examine all the gospels. While Peter stood in that corridor, a man confirmed what the servant girl said. So in the scene of Peter's second denial, both a girl and a man confronted him. And the crowd must have been drawn into it because Matthew 26:71 says the girl identified Peter "unto them that were there."

c) Peter's denial (v. 72)

"Again he denied with an oath, I do not know the man."

Peter was angry, embarrassed, frustrated, afraid, and confused. He had been trapped again. Now his denials were becoming more vehement. This time he told two lies: he lied when he claimed he didn't know Jesus, and he lied by taking an oath to his truthfulness. Taking an oath is swearing to the truth. The ultimate oath was to swear by the living God, which is what the high priest wants Jesus to do in verse 63: "I adjure thee by the living God, that thou tell us whether thou be the Christ, the Son of God." Peter made an oath—a personal pledge of truthfulness before God that he did not know Jesus.

Peter's second denial demonstrates his lack of trust in God. Why couldn't he speak the truth and commit himself to the care of the Lord? Because he didn't have spiritual strength. He was weak. Although he was the recipient of great spiritual privileges and experiences, he wasn't invincible. People who believe they are invulnerable to disaster because they know so much about the Bible and have experienced the blessings of God are actually the most vulnerable. That was true of Peter.

3. The third occasion (vv. 73-74a)

a) Peter's delay (v. 73a)

"After a while."

Both Matthew 26:73 and Mark 14:70 indicate that after his second denial Peter still hung around for a while, perhaps moving into the courtyard again. Luke 22:59 says he milled around for an hour after the second denial. Two hours have passed. The first two denials took place in the first hour, and now another hour has gone by. Peter couldn't bring himself to leave. No doubt by now he had drifted near the room in Caiaphas's wing of the house where Jesus' trial was being held. By this time the Sanhedrin and soldiers probably were spitting in Jesus' face and slapping Him (Matt. 26:67). Peter was nearby, perhaps able to see what was happening through the doorways and windows. He couldn't leave. Perhaps the screams of blasphemy and the beating Jesus was enduring held him there.

b) The crowd's accusation (v. 73*b*)

"Came unto him they that stood by, and said to Peter, Surely thou also art one of them; for thy speech betrayeth thee."

Peter's Galilean accent was readily distinguishable (Mark 14:70). Those who heard Peter speak confronted him. According to John 18:26 a spokesman in this group of people was a relative of Malchus, the high priest's servant whose ear Peter had cut off.

c) Peter's denial (v. 74*a*)

"Then began he to curse and to swear, saying, I know not the man."

Peter began to curse (Gk., *katanathematizō*). It's a strong word pronouncing death upon yourself if you're lying. It's like saying, "May God kill me and damn me if I'm not speaking the truth." That is taking the Lord's name in vain in the most serious way imaginable.

Verse 74 also says Peter swore (Gk., *omnuō*), which was a pledge of truthfulness. So on the positive side he pledged his truthfulness; on the negative side he called down the damning power of God on his own head if he wasn't telling the truth. Peter was so far from reality at that point that He lost all fear of God. He began with a single lie. Then to cover that up he lied twice. And now to cover that up he let loose with a flurry of curses. Verse 74 says he began to curse, which means he didn't do it once but continuously. Perhaps the crowd continued to accuse him and that's why he continued to curse and swear. The Lord was rejected by the world, sold by one of His disciples, and denied again and again by the leader of His own group. Isaiah 53:3 aptly calls Him a man of sorrows.

C. The Acknowledgment of Peter's Denials (v. 74*b*)

"Immediately the cock crowed."

That was the second time the cock crowed. The Lord's prediction came to pass. Luke 22:61 says that at the split second the cock crowed "the Lord turned, and looked upon Peter." Peter must have been able to see the Lord. Perhaps he was standing outside the window looking into the trial when the cock crowed. Or perhaps the trial had ended, and Jesus was being led away when He passed by Peter at the moment Peter denied Him for the third time. That look must have burned Peter's soul, causing the most excruciating pain he had ever experienced. Peter now understood he could never mistrust what Christ said. Burned indelibly in his heart was the evil of his sin. He would never forget what he had done. Yet I'm sure there was a measure of compassion and mercy in Jesus' look despite how much Peter's denials must have hurt Him, for soon Peter would be restored.

The collapse of Peter is frozen like a still picture, crystallized in stark imagery in a moment of time as the eyes of Peter met those of His Lord. How could Peter ever have sunk to such depth? He was spiritually self-confident—he believed he was invulnerable to danger. His insubordination, lack of prayer, and independence led to compromise. Whenever you believe you can handle any situation, that's when you can be sure you'll experience some situation you can't handle. That's where Peter was. During the darkest hour in human history, when hell was operating at full tilt, Peter was no match for the forces of the enemy and his demons. It wouldn't have been inconceivable at this point for Peter to go and hang himself, as Judas had. But he didn't.

VI. THE SINNER'S REMORSE (v. 75)

Despite all that Peter denied, the key to this message is his repentance. The true Peter is seen not in his denial but in his repentance. We don't wonder if Judas was a true believer because we know how his story ended—He hanged himself. Judas was not repentant. Peter didn't hang himself; he wept bitterly and then came back to be restored. Therein lies the difference between people like Judas and people like Peter. Both will sin, but one is repentant and will be restored while the other one is unrepentant and will be damned. Why is one repentant and not the other? Luke 22:31-32 is the key: Jesus said, "Simon, Simon, behold, Satan hath desired to have you, that he may sift you as wheat; but I have prayed for thee, that thy faith fail not." Do you know why Peter's faith didn't totally fail? Because the Lord prayed for him. The reason we stay saved is not the result of something we've done but of the sustaining power of the Lord to keep us saved. Jesus didn't keep Judas saved because he never was saved.

A. He Remembered (v. 75a)

"Peter remembered the words of Jesus, who said unto him, Before the cock crows, thou shalt deny me thrice."

B. He Left (v. 75b)

"He went out."

I'm glad none of the gospel writers tell us where Peter went or what he said—that was a private moment of repentance as Peter came to grips with his sin. It was a time for him to be alone with His Lord, whom he had so grossly offended.

C. He Wept (v. 75c)

"[He] wept bitterly."

Matthew used a strong expression in the Greek text (*eklausen pikrōs*), which means "to sob loudly."

We can learn a great lesson from Peter's experience. It wasn't until he saw the face of Jesus and remembered His words that he repented. Peter's sin didn't make him repent; his Savior made him repent. Here's the important principle: it's not our sins that make us weep and repent; it's seeing how we've offended our Savior that makes us repent. We always need to fix our eyes on Jesus (Heb. 12:1-2). Peter's sin didn't do anything positive for Peter—he would have kept on sinning. But when he saw Jesus and he remembered His words, his repentance was born out of a recognition of whom he sinned against. My objective in ministry is not to focus on encouraging you to turn from sin but to lift up our God of glory. It is only when you see the Lord Jesus Christ in all His glory that you can understand the heinous nature of sin.

In the agony of his repentance, Peter made his life right with the Lord. He was like Isaiah, who cried out to God, "I am a man of unclean lips" (Isa. 6:5). And like Isaiah, Peter was purified.

VII. THE SINNER'S RESTORATION (John 21:15-17)

John 21 describes a scene in Galilee. Peter had gone fishing with several of the disciples, shortly before the Lord appeared following His resurrection (vv. 3-4). Beginning in verse 15 Jesus asks Peter, "Simon, son of Jonah, lovest thou me?" In verses 16-17 He repeats that question two more times. In each case Peter answers by saying, "Thou knowest that I love thee." Why do you think the Lord gave him three opportunities? It's obvious—the Lord was restoring him. For each occasion of denial, Jesus allowed Peter to reaffirm his love. The Lord accepted Peter's testimony, and He restored Peter by saying, "Feed my lambs. . . . Feed my sheep. . . . Feed my sheep" (vv. 15-17). The Lord put Peter back on his feet and back in ministry. After that Peter became the great proclaimer of the gospel in the early church.

Conclusion

What a hopeful story! God is in the business of giving grace to sinners and restoring the fallen. He picks up even the person who has denied Him and shown himself to be weak, and puts him in a place of strength. I'm glad we have a God of forgiveness, aren't you?

Focusing on the Facts

1. What is the single greatest gift God could give us? Explain (see p. 132).
2. Explain Peter's boast (Matt. 26:33; see p. 133).
3. Why did the disciples fall asleep instead of praying (Matt. 26:40-41; see p. 134)?
4. Explain Peter's impulsiveness (Matt. 26:51; see p. 135).
5. Does John 18:12 contradict Matthew 26:57? Explain (see p. 136).
6. Explain how John inadvertently contributed to Peter's denials of Christ (see p. 137).
7. What did Peter do after gaining access to the courtyard of the high priest (Matt. 26:58)? What was he trying to do (see p. 138)?
8. Who confronted Peter first? How did that person know Peter was a follower of Christ (see p. 139)?
9. Why do we find variations of what the servant girl said to Peter in the different gospel accounts of that scene (see p. 139)?
10. Why did Peter deny Christ? Explain (see pp. 140-41).
11. What principle is illustrated by Peter's denials of Christ (see p. 141)?
12. What kind of response reveals a person's character? Explain (see pp. 141-42).
13. Why did Peter leave the fire in the courtyard and move to the corridor (see p. 142)?
14. What made Peter's second denial different from his first (Matt. 26:72; see p. 143)?
15. Describe Peter's third denial (Matt. 26:74; see pp. 144-45).
16. According to Luke 22:61, what happened the instant the cock crowed for the second time? Explain the significance of this event (see p. 145).
17. Why was Peter repentant? Why was Judas unrepentant (see p. 146)?
18. What made Peter repent? Explain (see p. 147).
19. Why did the Lord give Peter three opportunities to affirm his love (see p. 147)?

Pondering the Principles

1. As a Christian, God has given you the greatest gift He could possibly give you, and that is the forgiveness of your sins through the death of Christ on the cross. Thank Him right now for what His forgiveness means to you. Thank Him for what He is doing in your life today. Finally, thank Him for the things He will do in your life, and the fact that you will be with Him in heaven one day.

2. Analyze your spiritual preparedness. Are you like Peter, prepared for the big tests but unprepared for the small ones? Based on what you have learned from this lesson, what can you do to be better prepared for those small tests? Review the section on revealing character (see pp. 141-42). Our involuntary responses reveal our true character and its weaknesses. In Peter's case, what led to his failure in the small tests? How might you turn those weaknesses of Peter's character into strengths in your character? Commit yourself to building your spiritual character. As you do you will find your involuntary responses revealing your strengths and not your weaknesses.

3. Peter's repentance was born out of his recognition of Christ and his understanding that he sinned against Him. When you sin, what makes you repent? Do you repent out of sorrow for having sinned against Christ, or is it the result of knowing that as a believer you should repent of sin? Can the latter be true repentance if it isn't motivated by the former? Look up the following verses: Isaiah 6:5, Daniel 9:5-7, Micah 7:9, and Luke 15:17-20. What do each of those verses teach about the motivation for repentance? Read Psalm 51, and meditate on these verses that reveal David's repentant heart. Memorize the verses that are most meaningful to you. Use them to help motivate true repentance from your heart each time the Lord convicts you of sin.

Scripture Index

Topical Index

Moody Press, a ministry of the Moody Bible Institute, is designed for education, evangelization, and edification. If we may assist you in knowing more about Christ and the Christian life, please write us without obligation: Moody Press, c/o MLM, Chicago, Illinois 60610.